THE ART OF WAR

Niccolò Machiavelli

Translated by Henry Neville

DOVER PUBLICATIONS, INC.
Mineola, New York

Bibliographical Note

This Dover edition, first published in 2006, is a modernized republication of *The Art of War, in Seven Books*, excerpted from *The Works of the Famous Nicholas Machiavel, Citizen and Secretary of Florence*, translated from the original Italian by Henry Neville and first published in 1674. The appendix at the end of the book was taken from *The Arte of War*, Peter Whitehorne's translation of the same work which first appeared in 1560.

International Standard Book Number
ISBN-13: 978-0-486-44509-0
ISBN-10: 0-486-44509-7

Manufactured in the United States by Courier Corporation
44509705
www.doverpublications.com

Contents

Preface by Niccolò Machiavelli
Citizen and Secretary of Florence
on the books on the Art of War
to Lorenzo di Filippo Strozzi,
a gentleman of Florence

Many, Lorenzo, have held and still hold the opinion, that there is nothing which has less in common with another, and that is so dissimilar, as civilian life is from the military. Whence it is often observed, if anyone designs to avail himself of an enlistment in the army, that he soon changes, not only his clothes, but also his customs, his habits, his voice, and in the presence of any civilian custom, he goes to pieces; for I do not believe that any man can dress in civilian clothes who wants to be quick and ready for any violence; nor can that man have civilian customs and habits, who judges those customs to be effeminate and those habits not conducive to his actions; nor does it seem right to him to maintain his ordinary appearance and voice who, with his beard and cursing, wants to make other men afraid: which makes such an opinion in these times to be very true. But if they should consider the ancient institutions, they would not find matter more united, more in conformity, and which, of necessity, should be like to each other as much as these (civilian and military); for in all the arts that are established in a society for the sake of the common good of men, all those institutions created to (make people) live in fear of the laws and of God would be in vain, if their defense had not been provided for and which, if well arranged, will maintain not only these, but also those that are not well established. And so (on the contrary), good institutions without the help of the military are not much differently disordered than the habitation of a superb and regal palace, which, even though adorned with jewels and gold, if it is not roofed over will not have anything to protect it from the rain. And, if in any other institutions of a City

1

and of a Republic every diligence is employed in keeping men loyal, peaceful, and full of the fear of God, it is doubled in the military; for in what man ought the country look for greater loyalty than in that man who has to promise to die for her? In whom ought there to be a greater love of peace, than in him who can only be injured by war? In whom ought there to be a greater fear of God than in him who, undergoing infinite dangers every day, has more need for His aid? If these necessities in forming the life of the soldier are well considered, they are found to be praised by those who gave the laws to the Commanders and by those who were put in charge of military training, and followed and imitated with all diligence by others.

But because military institutions have become completely corrupt and far removed from the ancient ways, these sinister opinions have arisen which make the military hated and intercourse with those who train them avoided. And I, judging, by what I have seen and read, that it is not impossible to restore its ancient ways and return some form of past virtue to it, have decided not to let this leisure time of mine pass without doing something, to write what I know of the art of war, to the satisfaction of those who are lovers of the ancient deeds. And although it requires courage to treat of those matters of which others have made a profession, nonetheless, I do not believe that it is a mistake to occupy a position with words, which may, with greater presumption, have been occupied with deeds; for the errors which I should make in writing can be corrected without injury to anyone, but those which are made with deeds cannot be found out except by the ruin of the Commanders.

You, Lorenzo, will therefore consider the quality of these efforts of mine, and will give in your judgement of them that censure or praise which will appear to you to be merited. I send you these, as much as to show myself grateful for all the benefits I have received from you, although I will not include in them the (review) of this work of mine, as well as also, because being accustomed to honor similar works of those who shine because of their nobility, wealth, genius, and liberality, I know you do not have many equals in wealth and nobility, few in ingenuity, and no one in liberality.

FIRST BOOK

As I believe that it is possible for one to praise, without con-
cern, any man after he is dead since every reason and super-
vision for adulation is lacking, I am not apprehensive in praising
our own Cosimo Ruccelai, whose name is never remembered by
me without tears, as I have recognized in him those parts which
can be desired in a good friend among friends and in a citizen of
his country. For I do not know what pertained to him more than
to spend himself willingly, not excepting that courage of his, for
his friends, and I do not know of any enterprise that dismayed
him when he knew it was for the good of his country. And I confess freely not to have met among so many men whom I have
known and worked with, a man in whom there was a mind more
fired with great and magnificent things. Nor does one grieve
with the friends of another of his death, except for his having
been born to die young unhonored within his own home, without having been able to benefit anyone with that mind of his, for
one would know that no one could speak of him, except (to say)
that a good friend had died. It does not remain for us, however,
or for anyone else who, like us, knew him, to be able because of
this to keep the faith (since deeds do not seem to) to his laud-
able qualities. It is true however, that fortune was not so
unfriendly to him that it did not leave some brief memory of the
dexterity of his genius, as was demonstrated by some of his writ-
ings and compositions of amorous verses, in which (as he was
not in love) he (employed as an) exercise in order not to use his
time uselessly in his juvenile years, in order that fortune might
lead him to higher thoughts. Here, it can be clearly compre-

hended, that if his objective was exercise, how very happily he described his ideas, and how much he was honored in his poetry. Fortune, however, having deprived us of the use of so great a friend, it appears to me it is not possible to find any other better remedy than for us to seek to benefit from his memory, and recover from it any matter that was either keenly observed or wisely discussed. And as there is nothing of his more recent than the discussions which the Lord Fabrizio Colonna had with him in his gardens, where matters pertaining to war were discussed at length by that Lord, with (questions) keenly and prudently asked by Cosimo, it seemed proper to me having been present with other friends of ours, to recall him to memory, so that reading it, the friends of Cosimo who met there will renew in their minds the memory of his virtue, and another part grieving for not having been there, will learn in part of many things discussed wisely by a most sagacious man useful not only to the military way of life, but to the civilian as well. I will relate, therefore, how Fabrizio Colonna, when he returned from Lombardy where he had fought a long time gloriously for the Catholic King, decided to pass through Florence to rest several days in that City in order to visit His Excellency the Duke, and see again several gentlemen with whom he had been familiar in the past. Whence it appeared proper to Cosimo to invite him to a banquet in his gardens, not so much to show his generosity as to have reason to talk to him at length, and to learn and understand several things from him, according as one can hope to from such a man, for it appeared to him to give him an opportunity to spend a day discussing such matters as would satisfy his mind.

Fabrizio, therefore, came as planned, and was received by Cosimo together with several other loyal friends of his, among whom were Zanobi Buondelmonti, Battista Della Palla, and Luigi Alamanni, young men most ardent in the same studies and loved by him, whose good qualities, because they were also praised daily by himself, we will omit. Fabrizio, therefore, was honored according to the times and the place, with all the highest honors they could give him. As soon as the convivial pleasures were past and the table cleared and every arrangement of feasting finished, which, in the presence of great men and those who have their minds turned to honorable thoughts is soon accomplished, and because the day was long and the heat intense, Cosimo, in order to satisfy their desire better, judged it would be well to take the opportunity to escape the heat by leading them to the more secret and shadowy part of his garden: when they arrived there and chairs brought out, some sat on the grass which was most fresh in the place, some sat on chairs placed in those parts under the shadow of very high trees; Fabrizio praised the place as most delightful, and looking especially at the trees, he did not recognize one of them, and looked puzzled. Cosimo, becoming aware of this said: Perhaps you have no knowledge of some of these trees, but do not wonder about them, because here are some which were more widely known by the ancients than are those commonly seen today. And giving him the name of some and telling him that Bernardo, his grandfather, had worked hard in their culture, Fabrizio replied: I was thinking that it was what you said and this place and this study make me remember several Princes of the Kingdom, who delighted in their ancient culture and the shadow they cast. And stopping speaking of this, and somewhat upon himself as though in suspense, he added: If I did not think I would offend you, I would give you my opinion: but I do not believe in talking and discussing things with friends in this manner that I insult them. How much better would they have done (it is said with peace to everyone) to seek to imitate the ancients in the strong and rugged things, not in the soft and delicate, and in the things they did under the sun, not in the shadows, to adopt the honest and perfect ways of antiquity, not the false and corrupt; for while these practices were pleasing to my Romans, my country (without them) was ruined. To which Cosimo replied (but to avoid the necessity of having to repeat so many times who is speaking, and what the other adds, only the names of those speaking will be noted, without repeating the others). Cosimo, therefore, said: You have opened the way for a discussion which I desired, and I pray you to speak without regard, for I will question you without regard; and if, in questioning or in replying, I accuse or excuse anyone, it will not be for accusing or excusing, but to understand the truth from you.

Fabrizio: And I will be much content to tell you what I know of all that you ask me; whether it be true or not, I will leave to your judgement. And I will be grateful if you ask me, for I am about to learn as much from what you ask me, as you will from me replying to you, because many times a wise questioner causes one to consider many things and understand many others which, without having been asked, would never have been understood.

Cosimo: I want to return to what you first were saying, that my grandfather and those of yours had more wisely imitated the ancients in rugged things than in delicate ones, and I want to excuse my side because I will let you excuse the other (your side). I do not believe that in your time there was a man who disliked living as softly as he, and that he was so much a lover of that rugged life which you praise: nonetheless he recognized he could not practice it in his personal life, nor in that of his sons, having been born in so corrupted an age, where anyone who wanted to depart from the common usage would be deformed and despised by everyone. For if anyone in a naked state should thrash upon the sand under the highest sun, or upon the snow in the most icy months of winter, as did Diogenes, he would be considered mad. If anyone (like the Spartan) should raise his children on a farm, make them sleep in the open, go with head and feet bare, bathe in cold water in order to harden them to endure vicissitudes, so that they then might love life less and fear death less, he would be praised by few and followed by none. So that dismayed at these ways of living, he presently leaves the ways of the ancients, and in imitating antiquity, does only that which he can with little wonderment.

Fabrizio: You have excused him strongly in this part, and certainly you speak the truth: but I did not speak so much of these rugged ways of living, as of those other more human ways which have a greater conformity to the ways of living today, which I do not believe should have been difficult to introduce by one who is numbered among the Princes of a City. I will never forego my examples of my Romans. If their way of living should be examined, and the institutions in their Republic, there will be observed in her many things not impossible to introduce in a Society where there yet might be something of good.

Cosimo: What are those things similar to the ancients that you would introduce?

Fabrizio: To honor and reward virtue, not to have contempt for poverty, to esteem the modes and orders of military discipline, to constrain citizens to love one another, to live without factions, to esteem less the private than the public good, and other such things which could easily be added in these times. It is not difficult to persuade (people) to these ways, when one considers these at length and approaches them in the usual manner, for the truth will appear in such (examinations) that every common talent is capable of undertaking them. Anyone can arrange these things; (for example), one plants trees under the shadow of which he lives more happily and merrily than if he had not (planted them).

Cosimo: I do not want to reply to anything of what you have spoken, but I do want leave to give a judgment on these, which can be easily judged, and I shall address myself to you who accuse those who in serious and important actions are not imitators of the ancients, thinking that in this way I can more easily carry out my intentions. I should want, therefore, to know from you whence it arises that, on the one hand you condemn those who do not imitate the ancients in their actions, on the other hand, in matters of war which is your profession and in which you are judged to be excellent, it is not observed that you have employed any of the ancient methods, or those which have some similarity.

Fabrizio: You have come to the point where I expected you to, for what I said did not merit any other question, nor did I wish for any other. And although I am able to save myself with a simple excuse, nonetheless I want, for your greater satisfaction and mine, since the season (weather) allows it, to enter into a much longer discussion. Men who want to do something, ought first to prepare themselves with all industry, in order [when the opportunity is seen] to be prepared to achieve that which they have proposed. And whenever the preparations are undertaken cautiously, unknown to anyone, no one can be accused of negligence unless he is first discovered by the occasion; in which if it is not then successful, it is seen that either he has not sufficiently prepared himself, or that he has not in some part given thought to it. And as the opportunity has not come to me to be able to show the preparations I would make to bring the military to your ancient organization, and if I have not done so, I cannot be blamed either by you or by others. I believe this excuse is enough to respond to your accusation.

Cosimo: It would be enough if I was certain that the opportunity did not present itself.

Fabrizio: But because I know you could doubt whether this opportunity had come about or not, I want to discuss at length [if you will listen to me with patience] which preparations are necessary to be made first, what occasion needs to arise, what difficulty impedes the preparations from becoming beneficial and the occasion from arriving, and that this is [which appears a paradox] most difficult and most easy to do.

Cosimo: You cannot do anything more pleasing for me and for the others than this. But if it is not painful for you to speak, it will never be painful for us to listen. But as this discussion may be long, I want help from these, my friends, and with your permission, and they and I pray you one thing, that you do not become annoyed if we sometimes interrupt you with some opportune question.

Fabrizio: I am most content that you, Cosimo, with these other young people here, should question me, for I believe that young men will become more familiar with military matters, and will more easily understand what I have to say. The others, whose hair (head) is white and whose blood is icy, in part are enemies of war and in part incorrigible, as those who believe that the times and not the evil ways constrain men to live in such a fashion. So ask anything of me, with assurance and without regard; I desire this, as much because it will afford me a little rest, as because it will give me pleasure not to leave any doubts in your minds. I want to begin from your words, where you said to me that in war [which is my profession] I have not employed any of the ancient methods. Upon this I say, that this being a profession by which men of every time were not able to live

honestly, it cannot be employed as a profession except by a
Republic or a Kingdom; and both of these, if well established,
will never allow any of their citizens or subjects to employ it as
a profession: for he who practices it will never be judged to be
good, as to gain some usefulness from it at any time he must be
rapacious, deceitful, violent, and have many qualities, which of
necessity, do not make him good: nor can men who employ this
as a profession, the great as well as the least, be made otherwise,
for this profession does not provide for them in peace. Whence
they are obliged, either to hope that there will be no peace or to
gain so much for themselves in times of war, that they can provide for themselves in times of peace. And wherever one of
these two thoughts exists, it does not occur in a good man; for,
from the desire to provide for oneself in every circumstance,
robberies, violence and assassinations result, which such soldiers do to friends as well as to enemies: and from not desiring
peace, there arises those deceptions which Captains perpetrate
upon those whom they lead, because war hardens them: and
even if peace occurs frequently, it happens that the leaders,
being deprived of their stipends and of their licentious mode of
living, raise a flag of piracy, and without any mercy sack a
province.

Do you not have within the memory of events of your time,
many soldiers in Italy, finding themselves without employment
because of the termination of wars, gathered themselves into
very troublesome gangs, calling themselves companies, and
went about levying tribute on the towns and sacking the country, without there being any remedy able to be applied? Have
you not read how the Carthaginian soldiers, when the first war
they engaged in with the Romans under Matus and Spendius
was ended, tumultuously chose two leaders, and waged a more
dangerous war against the Carthaginians than that which they
had just concluded with the Romans? And in the time of our
fathers, Francesco Sforza, in order to be able to live honorably
(comfortably) in times of peace, not only deceived the Milanese,
in whose pay he was, but took away their liberty and became
their Prince. All the other soldiers of Italy, who have employed
the military as their particular profession, have been like this

man; and if, through their malignity, they have not become Dukes of Milan, so much more do they merit to be censured; for without such a return [if their lives were to be examined], they all have the same cares. Sforza, father of Francesco, constrained Queen Giovanna to throw herself into the arms of the King of Aragon, having abandoned her suddenly, and left her disarmed amid her enemies, only in order to satisfy his ambition of either levying tribute or taking the Kingdom. Braccio, with the same industry, sought to occupy the Kingdom of Naples, and would have succeeded, had he not been routed and killed at Aquilla. Such evils do not result from anything else other than the existence of men who employ the practice of soldiering as their own profession. Do you not have a proverb which strengthens my argument, which says: War makes robbers, and peace hangs them? For those who do not know how to live by another practice, and not finding any one who will support them in that, and not having so much virtue that they know how to come and live together honorably, are forced by necessity to roam the streets, and justice is forced to extinguish them.

Cosimo: You have made me turn this profession (art) of soldiering back almost to nothing, and I had supposed it to be the most excellent and most honorable of any: so that if you do not clarify this better, I will not be satisfied; for if it is as you say, I do not know whence arises the glory of Caesar, Pompey, Scipio, Marcellus, and of so many Roman Captains who are celebrated for their fame as the Gods.

Fabrizio: I have not yet finished discussing all that I proposed, which included two things: the one, that a good man was not able to undertake this practice because of his profession: the other, that a well established Republic or Kingdom would never permit its subjects or citizens to employ it for their profession. Concerning the first, I have spoken as much as has occurred to me: it remains for me to talk of the second, where I shall reply to this last question of yours, and I say that Pompey and Caesar, and almost all those Captains who were in Rome after the last Carthaginian war, acquired fame as valiant men, not as good men: but those who had lived before them acquired glory as valiant and good men: which results from the fact that these latter did not take up the practice of war as their profession; and those whom I named first as those who employed it as their profession. And while the Republic lived immaculately, no great citizen ever presumed by means of such a practice to enrich himself during (periods of) peace by breaking laws, despoiling the provinces, usurping and tyrannizing the country, and imposing himself in every way; nor did anyone of the lowest fortune think of violating the sacred agreement, adhere himself to any private individual, not fearing the Senate, or to perform any disgraceful act of tyranny in order to live at all times by the profession of war. But those who were Captains, being content with the triumph, returned with a desire for the private life; and those who were members (of the army) returned with a desire to lay down the arms they had taken up; and everyone returned to the art (trade or profession) by which they ordinarily lived; nor was there ever anyone who hoped to provide for himself by plunder and by means of these arts. A clear and evident example of this as it applies to great citizens can be found in the Regent Attilio, who, when he was captain of the Roman armies in Africa, and having almost defeated the Carthaginians, asked the Senate for permission to return to his house to look after his farms which were being spoiled by his laborers. Whence it is clearer than the sun, that if that man had practiced war as his profession, and by means of it thought to obtain some advantage for himself, having so many provinces which (he could) plunder, he would not have asked permission to return to take care of his fields, as each day he could have obtained more than the value of all his possessions. But as these good men, who do not practice war as their profession, do not expect to gain anything from it except hard work, danger, and glory, as soon as they are sufficiently glorious, desire to return to their homes and live from the practice of their own profession. As to men of lower status and gregarious soldiers, it is also true that every one voluntarily withdrew from such a practice, for when he was not fighting would have desired to fight, but when he was fighting wanted to be dismissed. Which illustrates the many ways, and especially in seeing that it was among the first privileges, that the Roman people gave to one of its Citizens, that he should not be constrained unwillingly to fight. Rome, therefore, while she was well organized [which it was up to the time of the Gracchi] did not have one soldier who had to take up this practice as a profession, and therefore had few bad ones, and these were severely punished. A well ordered City, therefore, ought to desire that this training for war ought to be employed in times of peace as an exercise, and in times of war as a necessity and for glory, and allow the public only to use it as a profession, as Rome did. And any citizen who has other aims in (using) such exercises is not good, and any City which governs itself otherwise, is not well ordered.

Cosimo: I am very much content and satisfied with what you have said up to now, and this conclusion which you have made pleases me greatly: and I believe it will be true when expected from a Republic, but as to Kings, I do not yet know why I should believe that a King would not want particularly to have around him those who take up such a practice as their profession.

Fabrizio: A well ordered Kingdom ought so much the more avoid such artifices, for these only are the things which corrupt the King and all the Ministers in a Tyranny. And do not, on the other side, tell me of some present Kingdom, for I will not admit them to be all well ordered Kingdoms; for Kingdoms that are well ordered do not give absolute (power to) Rule to their Kings, except in the armies, for only there is a quick decision necessary, and, therefore, he who (rules) there must have this unique power: in other matters, he cannot do anything without counsel, and those who counsel him have to fear those whom he may have near him who, in times of peace, desire war because they are unable to live without it. But I want to dwell a little longer on this subject, and look for a Kingdom totally good, but similar to those that exist today, where those who take up the profession of war for themselves still ought to be feared by the King, for the sinews of armies without any doubt are the infantry. So that if a King does not organize himself in such a way that his infantry in time of peace are content to return to their homes and live from the practice of their own professions, it must happen of necessity that he will be ruined; for there is not to be found a more dangerous infantry than that which is

composed of those who make the waging of war their profession; for you are forced to make war always, or pay them always,
or to risk the danger that they take away the Kingdom from you.
To make war always is not possible: (and) one cannot pay always;
and, hence, that danger is run of losing the State. My Romans
[as I have said], as long as they were wise and good, never permitted that their citizens should take up this practice as their
profession, notwithstanding that they were able to raise them at
all times, for they made war at all times: but in order to avoid
the harm which this continuous practice of theirs could do to
them, since the times did not change, they changed the men,
and kept turning men over in their legions so that every fifteen
years they always completely re-manned them: and thus they
desired men in the flower of their age, which is from eighteen
to thirty five years, during which time their legs, their hands,
and their eyes, worked together, nor did they expect that their
strength should decrease in them, or that malice should grow in
them, as they did in corrupt times.

Ottavianus first, and then Tiberius, thinking more of their
own power than the public usefulness, in order to rule over the
Roman people more easily, began to disarm them and to keep
the same armies continually at the frontiers of the Empire. And
because they did not think it sufficient to hold the Roman
People and the Senate in check, they instituted an army called
the Praetorian (Guard), which was kept near the walls of Rome
in a fort adjacent to that City. And as they now began freely to
permit men assigned to the army to practice military matters as
their profession, there soon resulted that these men became
insolent, and they became formidable to the Senate and damag-
ing to the Emperor. Whence there resulted that many men were
killed because of their insolence, for they gave the Empire and
took it away from anyone they wished, and it often occurred that
at one time there were many Emperors created by the several
armies. From which state of affairs proceeded first the division
of the Empire and finally its ruin. Kings ought, therefore, if they
want to live securely, have their infantry composed of men, who,
when it is necessary for him to wage war, will willingly go forth
to it for love of him, and afterwards when peace comes, more

willingly return to their homes; which will always happen if he
selects men who know how to live by a profession other than
this. And thus he ought to desire, with the coming of peace, that
his Princes return to governing their people, gentlemen to the
cultivation of their possessions, and the infantry to their particular arts (trades or professions); and everyone of these will willingly make war in order to have peace, and will not seek to
disturb the peace to have war.

Cosimo: Truly, this reasoning of yours appears to me well
considered: nonetheless, as it is almost contrary to what I have
thought up to now, my mind is not yet purged of every doubt.
For I see many Lords and Gentlemen who provide for themselves in times of peace through the training for war, as do your
equals who obtain provisions from Princes and the Community.
I also see almost all the men at arms remaining in the garrisons
of the city and of the fortresses. So that it appears to me that
there is a long time of peace for everyone.

Fabrizio: I do not believe that you believe this, that everyone
has a place in time of peace; for other reasons can be cited for
their being stationed there, and the small number of people who
remain in the places mentioned by you will answer your question. What is the proportion of infantry needed to be employed
in time of war to that in peace? for while the fortresses and the
city are garrisoned in times of peace, they are much more garrisoned in times of war; to this should be added the soldiers kept
in the field who are a great number, but all of whom are released
in time of peace. And concerning the garrisons of States, who
are a small number, Pope Julius and you have shown how much
they are to be feared who do not know any other profession than
war, as you have taken them out of your garrisons because of
their insolence, and placed the Swiss there, who are born and
raised under the laws and are chosen by the community in an
honest election; so do not say further that in peace there is a
place for every man. As to the men at arms continued in their
enlistment in peace time, the answer appears more difficult.
nonetheless, whoever considers everything well, will easily find
the answer, for this thing of keeping on the men at arms is a corrupt thing and not good. The reason is this; as there are men

who do not have any art (trade or profession), a thousand evils will arise every day in those States where they exist, and especially so if they were to be joined by a great number of companions: but as they are few, and unable by themselves to constitute an army, they therefore, cannot do any serious damage. nonetheless, they have done so many times, as I said of Francesco and of Sforza, his father, and of Braccio of Perugia. So I do not approve of this custom of keeping men at arms, both because it is corrupt and because it can cause great evils.

Cosimo: Would you do without them?, or if you keep them, how would you do so?

Fabrizio: By means of an ordinance, not like those of the King of France, because they are as dangerous and insolent as ours, but like those of the ancients, who created horsemen (cavalry) from their subjects, and in times of peace sent them back to their homes to live from the practice of their own profession, as I shall discuss at length before I finish this discussion. So, if this part of the army can now live by such a practice even when there is peace, it stems from a corrupt order. As to the provisions that are reserved for me and the other leaders, I say to you that this likewise is a most corrupt order, for a wise Republic ought not to give them to anyone, rather it ought to employ its citizens as leaders in war, and in time of peace desire that they return to their professions. Thus also, a wise King ought not to give (provisions) to them, or if he does give them, the reasons ought to be either as a reward for some excellent act, or in order to avail himself of such a man in peace as well as in war. And because you have mentioned me, I want the example to include me, and I say I have never practiced war as a profession, for my profession is to govern my subjects, and defend them, and in order to defend them, I must love peace but know how to make war; and my King does not reward and esteem me so much for what I know of war, as because I know also how to counsel him in peace. Any King ought not, therefore, to want to have next to him anyone who is not thusly constituted, if he is wise and wants to govern prudently; for if he has around him either too many lovers of peace or too many lovers of war, they will cause him to err. I cannot, in this first discussion of mine and according to my suggestion, say otherwise, and if this is not enough for you, you must seek one which satisfies you better. You can begin to recognize how much difficulty there is in bringing the ancient methods into modern wars, and what preparations a wise man must make, and what opportunities he can hope for to put them into execution. But little by little you will know these things better if the discussion on bringing any part of the ancient institutions to the present order of things does not weary you.

Cosimo: If we first desired to hear your discussion of these matters, truly what you have said up to now redoubles that desire. We thank you, therefore, for what we have had and ask you for the rest.

Fabrizio: Since this is your pleasure, I want to begin to treat of this matter from the beginning being able in that way to demonstrate it more fully, so that it may be better understood. The aim of those who want to make war is to be able to combat in the field with every (kind) of enemy, and to be able to win the engagement. To want to do this, they must raise an army. In raising an army, it is necessary to find men, arm them, organize them, train them in small and large (battle) orders, lodge them, and expose them to the enemy afterwards, either at a standstill or while marching. All the industry of war in the field is placed in these things, which are the more necessary and honored (in the waging of war). And if one does well in offering battle to the enemy, all the other errors he may make in the conduct of the war are supportable: but if he lacks this organization, even though he be valiant in other particulars, he will never carry on a war to victory (and honor). For, as one engagement that you win cancels out every other bad action of yours, so likewise, when you lose one, all the things you have done well before become useless. Since it is necessary, therefore, first to find men, you must come to the Deletto (Draft) of them, as thus the ancients called it, and which we call Scelta (Selection): but in order to call it by a more honored name, I want us to preserve the name of Deletto. Those who have drawn up regulations for war want men to be chosen from temperate countries as they have spirit and are prudent; for warm countries give rise to men who are prudent but not spirited, and cold (countries) to men who are spirited but not prudent. This regulation is drawn up well for one who is the Prince of all the world, and is therefore permitted to draw men from those places that appear best to him: but wanting to draw up a regulation that anyone can use, one must say that every Republic and every Kingdom ought to take soldiers from their own country, whether it is hot, cold, or temperate. For, from ancient examples, it is seen that in every country, good soldiers are made by training; because where nature is lacking, industry supplies it, which, in this case, is worth more than nature: And selecting them from another place cannot be called Deletto, because Deletto means to say to take the best of a province, and to have the power to select as well those who do not want to fight as those who do want to. This Deletto therefore, cannot be made unless the places are subject to you; for you cannot take whoever you want in the countries that are not yours, but you need to take those who want to come.

Cosimo: And of those who want to come, it can even be said, that they turn and leave you, and because of this, it can then be called a Deletto.

Fabrizio: In a certain way, you say what is true: but consider the defects that such as Deletto has in itself, for often it happens that it is not a Deletto. The first thing (to consider), is that those who are not your subjects and do not willingly want to fight, are not of the best, rather they are of the worst of a province; for if any are troublesome, idle, without restraint, without religion, subject to the rule of the father, blasphemous, gamblers, and in every way badly brought up, they are those who want to fight, (and) these habits cannot be more contrary to a true and good military life. When there are so many of such men offered to you that they exceed the number you had designated, you can select them; but if the material is bad, it is impossible for the Deletto to be good: but many times it happens that they are not so many as (are needed) to fill the number you require: so that being forced to take them all, it results that it can no longer be called the making of a Deletto, but in enlisting of infantry. The armies of Italy and other places are raised today with these evils, except in Germany, where no one is enlisted by command of the Prince, but according to the wishes of those who want to fight.

Think, therefore, what methods of those ancients can now be introduced in an army of men put together by similar means.

Cosimo: What means should be taken therefore?

Fabrizio: What I have just said: select them from your own subjects, and with the authority of the Prince.

Cosimo: Would you introduce any ancient form in those thus selected?

Fabrizio: You know well it would be so; if it is a Principality, he who should command should be their Prince or an ordinary Lord; or if it is a Republic, a citizen who for the time should be Captain: otherwise it is difficult to do the thing well.

Cosimo: Why?

Fabrizio: I will tell you in time: for now, I want this to suffice for you, that it cannot be done well in any other way.

Cosimo: If you have, therefore, to make ibis Deletto in your country, whence do you judge it better to draw them, from the City or the Countryside?

Fabrizio: Those who have written of this all agree that it is better to select them from the Countryside, as they are men accustomed to discomfort, brought up on hard work, accustomed to be in the sun and avoid the shade, know how to handle the sword, dig a ditch, carry a load, and are without cunning or malice. But on this subject, my opinion would be, that as soldiers are of two kinds, afoot and on horseback, that those afoot be selected from the Countryside, and those on horseback from the City.

Cosimo: Of what age would you draw them?

Fabrizio: If I had to raise an (entirely) new army, I would draw them from seventeen to forty years of age; if the army already exists and I had to replenish it, at seventeen years of age always.

Cosimo: I do not understand this distinction well.

Fabrizio: I will tell you: if I should have to organize an army where there is none, it would be necessary to select all those men who were more capable, as long as they were of military age, in order to instruct them as I would tell them: but if I should have to make the Deletto in places where the army was (already) organized, in order to supplement it, I would take those of seventeen years of age, because the others having been taken for some time would have been selected and instructed.

Cosimo: Therefore you would want to make an ordinance similar to that which exists in our countries.

Fabrizio: You say well: it is true that I would arm them, captain them, train them, and organize them, in a way which I do not know whether or not you have organized them similarly.

Cosimo: Therefore you praise the ordinance?

Fabrizio: Why would you want me to condemn it?

Cosimo: Because many wise men have censured it.

Fabrizio: You say something contrary, when you say a wise man censured the ordinance: for he can be held a wise man and to have censured them wrongly.

Cosimo: The wrong conclusion that he has made will always cause us to have such a opinion.

Fabrizio: Watch out that the defect is not yours, but his: as that which you recognized before this discussion furnishes proof.

Cosimo: You do a most gracious thing. But I want to tell you that you should be able to justify yourself better in that of which those men are accused. These men say thusly: either that it is useless and our trusting in it will cause us to lose the State: or it is of virtue, and he who governs through it can easily deprive her of it. They cite the Romans, who by their own arms lost their liberty: They cite the Venetians and the King of France, of whom they say that the former, in order not to obey one of its Citizens employed the arms of others, and the King disarmed his People so as to be able to command them more easily. But they fear the uselessness of this much more; for which uselessness they cite two principal reasons: the one, because they are inexpert; the other, for having to fight by force: because they say that they never learn anything from great men, and nothing good is ever done by force.

Fabrizio: All the reasons that you mention are from men who are not far sighted, as I shall clearly show. And first, as to the uselessness, I say to you that no army is of more use than your own, nor can an army of your own be organized except in this way. And as there is no debating over this, which all the examples of ancient history does for us, I do not want to lose time over it. And because they cite inexperience and force, I say [as it is true] that inept experience gives rise to little spirit (enthusiasm) and force makes for discontent: but experience and enthusiasm gains for themselves the means for arming, training, and organizing them, as you will see in the first part of this discussion. But as to force, you must understand that as men are brought to the army by commandment of the Prince, they have to come, whether it is entirely by force or entirely voluntarily: for if it were entirely from desire, there would not be a Deletto as only a few of them would go; so also, the (going) entirely by force would produce bad results; therefore, a middle way ought to be taken where neither the entirely forced or entirely voluntarily (means are used), but they should come, drawn by the regard they have for the Prince, where they are more afraid of his anger then the immediate punishment: and it will always happen that there will be a compulsion mixed with willingness, from which that discontent cannot arise which causes bad effects. Yet I do not claim that an army thus constituted cannot be defeated; for many times the Roman armies were overcome, and the army of Hannibal was defeated: so that it can be seen that no army can be so organized that a promise can be given that it cannot be routed. These wise men of yours, therefore, ought not measure this uselessness from having lost one time, but to believe that just as they can lose, so too they can win and remedy the cause of the defeat. And if they should look into this, they will find that it would not have happened because of a defect in the means, but of the organization which was not sufficiently perfect. And, as I have said, they ought to provide for you, not by censuring the organization, but by correcting it: as to how this ought to be done, you will come to know little by little.

As to being apprehensive that such organization will not deprive you of the State by one who makes himself a leader, I reply, that the arms carried by his citizens or subjects, given to them by laws and ordinances, never do him harm, but rather are always of some usefulness, and preserve the City uncorrupted for a longer time by means of these (arms), than without (them). Rome remained free four hundred years while armed: Sparta eight hundred: Many other Cities have been disarmed, and have been free less than forty years; for Cities have need of arms, and if they do not have arms of their own, they hire them from foreigners, and the arms of foreigners more readily do harm to the public good than their own; for they are easier to corrupt, and a citizen who becomes powerful can more readily avail himself, and can also manage the people more readily as he has to oppress men who are disarmed. In addition to this, a City ought to fear two enemies more than one. One which avails itself of foreigners immediately has to fear not only its citizens, but the foreigners that it enlists; and, remembering what I told you a short while ago of Francesco Sforza, (you will see that) that fear ought to exist. One which employs its own arms, has not other fear except of its own Citizens. But of all the reasons which can be given, I want this one to serve me, that no one ever established any Republic or Kingdom who did not think that it should be defended by those who lived there with arms: and if the Venetians had been as wise in this as in their other institutions, they would have created a new world Kingdom; but who so much more merit censure, because they had been the first who were armed by their founders. And not having dominion on land, they armed themselves on the sea, where they waged war with virtue, and with arms in hand enlarged their country. But when the time came when they had to wage war on land to defend Venice and where they ought to have sent their own citizens to fight (on land), they enlisted as their captain (a foreigner), the Marquis of Mantua. This was the sinister course which prevented them from rising to the skies and expanding. And they did this in the belief that, as they knew how to wage war at sea, they should not trust themselves in waging it on land; which was an unwise belief (distrust), because a Sea captain, who is accustomed to combat with winds, water, and men, could more easily become a Captain on land where the combat is with men only, than a land Captain become a sea one. And my Romans, knowing how to combat on land and not on the sea, when the war broke out with the Carthaginians who were powerful on the sea, did not enlist Greeks or Spaniards experienced at sea, but imposed that change on those citizens they sent (to fight) on land, and they won. If they did this in order that one of their citizens should not become Tyrant, it was a fear that was given little consideration; for, in addition to the other reasons mentioned a short while ago concerning such a proposal, if a citizen (skilled) in (the use of) arms at sea had never been made a Tyrant in a City situated in the sea, so much less would he be able to do this if he were (skilled) in (the use of arms) on land. And, because of this, they ought to have seen that arms in the hands of their own citizens could not create Tyrants, but the evil institutions of a Government are those which cause a City to be tyrannized; and, as they had a good Government, did not have to fear arms of their own citizens. They took an imprudent course, therefore, which was the cause of their being deprived of much glory and happiness. As to the error which the King of France makes in not having his people disciplined to war, from what has been cited from examples previously mentioned, there is no one [devoid of some particular passion of theirs] who does not judge this defect to be in the Republic, and that this negligence alone is what makes it weak. But I have made too great a digression and have gotten away from my subject: yet I have done this to answer you and to show you, that no reliance can be had on arms other than one's own, and ones own arms cannot be established otherwise than by way of an ordinance, nor can forms of armies be introduced in any place, nor military discipline instituted. If you have read the arrangements which the first Kings made in Rome, and most especially of Servius Tullus, you will find that the institution of classes is none other than an arrangement to be able quickly to put together an army for the defense of that City. But turning to our Deletto, I say again, that having to replenish an established (old) organization, I would take the seventeen year olds, but having to create a new one, I would take them of every age between seventeen and forty in order to avail myself of them quickly.

Cosimo: Would you make a difference of what profession (art) you would choose them from?

Fabrizio: These writers do so, for they do not want that bird hunters, fishermen, cooks, procurers, and anyone who makes amusement his calling should be taken, but they want that, in addition to tillers of the soil, smiths and blacksmiths, carpenters, butchers, hunters, and such like, should be taken. But I would make little difference in conjecturing from his calling how good the man may be, but how much I can use him with the greatest usefulness. And for this reason, the peasants, who are accustomed to working the land, are more useful than anyone else, for of all the professions (arts), this one is used more than any other in the army: After this, are the forgers (smiths), carpenters, blacksmiths, shoemakers; of whom it is useful to have many, for their skills succeed in many things, as they are a very good thing for a soldier to have, from whom you draw double service.

Cosimo: How are those who are or are not suitable to fight chosen?

Fabrizio: I want to talk of the manner of selecting a new organization in order to make it afterwards into an army; which yet also apply in the discussion of the selection that should be made in re-manning an old (established) organization. I say, therefore, that how good the man is that you have to select as a soldier is recognized either from his experience, shown by some excellent deeds of his, or by conjecture. The proof of virtue cannot be found in men who are newly selected, and who never before have been selected; and of the former, few or none are found in an organization which is newly established. It is necessary, therefore, lacking experience to have recourse to conjecture, which is derived from their age, profession, and physical appearance. The first two have been discussed: it remains to talk of the third. And yet I say that some have wanted that the soldier be big, among whom was Pyrrhus: Some others have chosen them only from the strength of the body, as Caesar did: which strength of body is conjectured from the composition of the members and the gracefulness of aspect. And yet some of those who write say that he should have lively and merry eyes, a nervy neck, a large breast, muscular arms, long fingers, a small stomach, round hips, sleek legs and feet: which parts usually render a man strong and agile, which are the two things sought above everything else in a soldier. He ought, above all, to have regard for his habits and that there should be in him a (sense of) honesty and shame, otherwise there will be selected only an instrument of trouble and a beginning of corruption; for there is no one who believes that in a dishonest education and in a brutish mind, there can exist some virtue which in some part may be praiseworthy. Nor does it appear to me superfluous, rather I believe it necessary, in order for you to understand better the importance of this selection, to tell you the method that the Roman Consuls at the start of their Magistracy observed in selecting the Roman legions. In which Deletto, because those who had to be selected were to be a mixture of new and veteran men [because of the continuing wars], they proceeded from experience with regard to the old (veteran) men, and from conjecture with regard to the new. And this ought to be noted, that these Deletti are made, either for immediate training and use, or for future employment.

I have talked, and will talk, of those that are made for future employment, because my intention is to show you how an army can be organized in countries where there is no military (organization), in which countries I cannot have Deletti in order to make use of them. But in countries where it is the custom to call out armies, and by means of the Prince, these (Deletti) exist, as was observed at Rome and is today observed among the Swiss. For in these Deletti, if they are for the (selection of) new men, there are so many others accustomed to being under military orders, that the old (veteran) and new, being mixed together, make a good and united body. Notwithstanding this, the Emperors, when they began to hold fixed the (term of service of the) soldiers, placed new men in charge over the soldiers, whom they called Tironi, as teachers to train them, as is seen in the life of the Emperor Maximus: which thing, while Rome was free, was instituted, not in the army, but within the City: and as the military exercises where the young men were trained were in the City, there resulted that those then chosen to go to war, being accustomed in the method of mock warfare, could easily adapt themselves to real war. But afterwards, when these Emperors discontinued these exercises, it was necessary to employ the methods I have described to you. Arriving, therefore, at the methods of the Roman Selection, I say that, as soon

as the Roman Consuls, on whom was imposed the carrying on
of the war, had assumed the Magistracy, in wanting to organize
their armies [as it was the custom that each of them had two
legions of Roman men, who were the nerve (center) of their
armies], created twenty four military Tribunes, proposing six for
each legion, who filled that office which today is done by those
whom we call Constables. After they had assembled all the
Roman men adept at carrying arms, and placed the Tribunes of
each legion apart from each of the others. Afterwards, by lot
they drew the Tribes, from which the first Selection was to be
made, and of that Tribe they selected four of their best men,
from whom one was selected by the Tribunes of the first legion,
and of the other three, one was selected by the Tribunes of the
second legion; of the other two, one was selected by the
Tribunes of the third, and that last belonged to the fourth
legion. After these four, four others were selected, of whom the
first man was selected by the Tribunes of the second legion,
the second by those of the third, the third by those of the fourth,
the fourth remained to the first. After, another four were chosen: the first man was selected by the (Tribunes of the) third
(legion), the second by the fourth, the third by the first, the
fourth remained to the second. And thus this method of selection changed successively, so that the selection came to be
equal, and the legions equalized. And as we said above, this was
done where the men were to be used immediately: and as it was
formed of men of whom a good part were experienced in real
warfare, and everyone in mock battles, this Deletto was able to
be based on conjecture and experience. But when a new army
was to be organized and the selection made for future employment, this Deletto cannot be based except on conjecture, which
is done by age and physical appearance.

Cosimo: I believe what you have said is entirely true: but
before you pass on to other discussion, I want to ask about one
thing which you have made me remember, when you said that
the Deletto which should be made where these men are not
accustomed to fighting should be done by conjecture: for I have
heard our organization censured in many of its parts, and especially as to number; for many say that a lesser number ought to

be taken, of whom those that are drawn would be better and the selection better, as there would not be as much hardship imposed on the men, and some reward given them, by means of which they would be more content and could be better commanded. Whence I would like to know your opinion on this part, and if you preferred a greater rather than a smaller number, and what methods you would use in selecting both numbers.

Fabrizio: Without doubt the greater number is more desirable and more necessary than the smaller: rather, to say better, where a great number is not available, a perfect organization cannot be made, and I will easily refute all the reasons cited in favor of this. I say, therefore, first, that where there are many people, as there are for example in Tuscany, does not cause you to have better ones, or that the Deletto is more selective; for desiring in the selection of men to judge them on the basis of experience, only a very few would probably be found in that country who would have had this experience, as much because few have been in a war, as because of those few who have been, very few have ever been put to the test, so that because of this they merit to be chosen before the others: so that whoever is in a similar situation should select them, must leave experience to one side and take them by conjecture: and if I were brought to such a necessity, I would want to see, if twenty young men of good physical appearance should come before me, with what rule I ought to take some or reject some: so that without doubt I believe that every man will confess that it is a much smaller error to take them all in arming and training them, being unable to know (beforehand) which of them are better, and to reserve to oneself afterwards to make a more certain Deletto where, during the exercises with the army, those of greater courage and vitality may be observed. So that, considering everything, the selection in this case of a few in order to have them better, is entirely false. As to causing less hardship to the country and to the men, I say that the ordinance, whether it is bad or insufficient, does not cause any hardship: for this order does not take men away from their business, and does not bind them so that they cannot go to carry out their business, because it only obliges them to come together for training on their free days, which proposition does not do any harm either to the country or the men; rather, to the young, it ought to be delightful, for where, on holidays they remain basely indolent in their hangouts, they would now attend these exercises with pleasure, for the drawing of arms, as it is a beautiful spectacle, is thus delightful to the young men. As to being able to pay (more to) the lesser number, and thereby keeping them more content and obedient, I reply, that no organization of so few can be made, who are paid so continually, that their pay satisfies them. For instance, if an army of five thousand infantry should be organized, in wanting to pay them so that it should be believed they would be contented, they must be given at least ten thousand ducats a month. To begin with, this number of infantry is not enough to make an army, and the payment is unendurable to a State; and on the other hand, it is not sufficient to keep the men content and obligated to respect your position. So that in doing this although much would be spent, it would provide little strength, and would not be sufficient to defend you, or enable you to undertake any enterprise. If you should give them more, or take on more, so much more impossible would it be for you to pay them: if you should give them less, or take on fewer, so much less would be content and so much less useful would they be to you. Therefore, those who consider such things are either useless or impossible. But it is indeed necessary to pay them when they are levied to send to war.

But even if such an arrangement should give some hardship to those enrolled in it in times of peace, which I do not see, they are still recompensed by all those benefits which an army established in a City brings; for without them, nothing is secure. I conclude that whoever desires a small number in order to be able to pay them, or for any other reason cited by you, does not know (what he is doing); for it will also happen, in my opinion, that any number will always diminish in your hands, because of the infinite impediments that men have; so that the small number will succeed at nothing. However, when you have a large organization, you can at your election avail yourself of few or of many. In addition to this, it serves you in fact and reputation, for the large number will always give you reputation. Moreover, in creating the organization, in order to keep men trained, if you enroll a small number of men in many countries, and the armies are very distant from each other, you cannot without the gravest injury to them assemble them for (joint) exercises, and without this training the organization is useless, as will be shown in its proper place.

Cosimo: What you have said is enough on my question: but I now desire that you resolve another doubt for me. There are those who say that such a multitude of armed men would cause confusion, trouble, and disorder in the country.

Fabrizio: This is another vain opinion for the reason I will tell you. These organized under arms can cause disorders in two ways: either among themselves, or against others; both of these can be obviated where discipline by itself should not do so: for as to troubles among themselves, the organization removes them, not brings them up, because in the organization you give them arms and leaders. If the country where you organize them is so unwarlike that there are not arms among its men, and so united that there are no leaders, such an organization will make them more ferocious against the foreigner, but in no way will make it more disunited, because men well organized, whether armed or unarmed, fear the laws, and can never change, unless the leaders you give them cause a change; and I will later tell you the manner of doing this. But if the country where you have organized an army is warlike and disunited, this organization alone is reason enough to unite them, for these men have arms and leaders for themselves: but the arms are useless for war, and the leaders causes of troubles; but this organization gives them arms useful for war, and leaders who will extinguish troubles; for as soon as someone is injured in that country, he has recourse to his (leader) of the party, who, to maintain his reputation, advises him to avenge himself, (and) not to remain in peace. The public leader does the contrary. So that by this means, the causes for trouble are removed, and replaced by those for union; and provinces which are united but effeminate (unwarlike) lose their usefulness but maintain the union, while those that are disunited and troublesome remain united; and that disordinate ferocity which they usually employ, is turned to public usefulness.

As to desiring that they do us injury against others, it should be kept in mind that they cannot do this except by the leaders who govern them. In desiring that the leaders do not cause disorders, it is necessary to have care that they do not acquire too much authority over them. And you have to keep in mind that this authority is acquired either naturally or by accident: And as to nature, it must be provided that whoever is born in one place is not put in charge of men enrolled in another place, but is made a leader in those places where he does not have any natural connections. As to accidents, the organization should be such that each year the leaders are exchanged from command to command; for continuous authority over the same men generates so much unity among them, which can easily be converted into prejudice against the Prince. As to these exchanges being useful to those who have employed them, and injurious to those who have not observed them, is known from the example of the Kingdom of Assyria and from the Empire of the Romans, in which it is seen that the former Kingdom endured a thousand years without tumult and without civil war; which did not result from anything else than the exchanges of those Captains, who were placed in charge of the care of the armies, from place to place every year. Nor, for other reasons, (did it result) in the Roman Empire; once the blood (race) of Caesar was extinguished, so many civil wars arose among the Captains of the armies, and so many conspiracies of the above mentioned Captains against the Emperors, resulting from the continuing of those Captains in their same Commands. And if any of those Emperors, and any who later held the Empire by reputation, such as Hadrian, Marcus, Severus, and others like them, would have observed such happenings, and would have introduced this custom of exchanging Captains in that Empire, without doubt they would have made it more tranquil and lasting; for the Captains would have had fewer opportunities for creating tumults, and the Emperors fewer causes to fear them, and the Senate, when there was a lack in the succession, would have had more authority in the election of Emperors, and consequently, better conditions would have resulted. But the bad customs of men, whether from ignorance or little diligence, or from examples of good or bad, are never put aside.

Cosimo: I do not know if, with my question, I have gone outside the limits you set; for from the Deletto we have entered into another discussion, and if I should not be excused a little, I shall believe I merit some reproach.

Fabrizio: This did us no harm; for all this discussion was necessary in wanting to discuss the Organization (of an Army), which, being censured by many, it was necessary to explain it, if it is desired that this should take place before the Deletto. And before I discuss the other parts, I want to discuss the Deletto for men on horseback. This (selection) was done by the ancients from among the more wealthy, having regard both for the age and quality of the men, selecting three hundred for each legion: so that the Roman cavalry in every Consular army did not exceed six hundred.

Cosimo: Did you organize the cavalry in order to train them at home and avail yourself of them in the future?

Fabrizio: Actually it is a necessity and cannot be done otherwise, if you want to have them take up arms for you, and not to want to take them away from those who make a profession of them.

Cosimo: How would you select them?

Fabrizio: I would imitate the Romans: I would take the more wealthy, and give them leaders in the same manner as they are given to others today, and I would arm them, and train them.

Cosimo: Would it be well to give these men some provision?

Fabrizio: Yes, indeed: but only as much as is necessary to take care of the horse; for, as it brings an expense to your subjects, they could complain of you. It would be necessary, therefore, to pay them for the horse and its upkeep.

Cosimo: How many would you make? How would you arm them?

Fabrizio: You pass into another discussion. I will tell you in its place, which will be when I have said how the infantry ought to be armed, and how they should prepare for an engagement.

SECOND BOOK

I believe that it is necessary, once the men are found, to arm them; and in wanting to do this, I believe it is necessary to examine what arms the ancients used, and from them select the best. The Romans divided their infantry into the heavily and lightly armed. The light armed they gave the name Veliti. Under this name they included all those who operated with the sling, cross-bow, and darts: and the greater part of them carried a helmet (head covering) and a shield on the arm for their defense. These men fought outside the regular ranks, and apart from the heavy armor, which was a Casque that came up to the shoulders, they also carried a Cuirass which, with the skirt, came down to the knees, and their arms and legs were covered by shin-guards and bracelets; they also carried a shield on the arm, two arms in length and one in width, which had an iron hoop on it to be able to sustain a blow, and another underneath, so that in rubbing on the ground, it should not be worn out. For attacking, they had cinched on their left side a sword of an arm and a half length, and a dagger on the right side. They carried a spear, which they called Pilus, and which they hurled at the enemy at the start of a battle. These were the important Roman arms, with which they conquered the world. And although some of the ancient writers also gave them, in addition to the aforementioned arms, a shaft in the hand in the manner of a spit, I do not know how a staff can be used by one who holds a shield, for in managing it with two hands it is impeded by the shield, and he cannot do anything worthwhile with one hand because of its heaviness. In addition to this, to combat in the ranks with the staff (as arms)

31

is useless, except in the front rank where there is ample space to deploy the entire staff, which cannot be done in the inner ranks, because the nature of the battalions [as I will tell you in their organization] is to press its ranks continually closer together, as this is feared less, even though inconvenient, than for the ranks to spread further apart, where the danger is most apparent. So that all the arms which exceed two arms in length are useless in tight places; for if you have a staff and want to use it with both hands, and handled so that the shield should not annoy you, you cannot attack an enemy with it who is next to you. If you take it in one hand in order to serve yourself of the shield, you cannot pick it up except in the middle, and there remains so much of the staff in the back part, that those who are behind impede you in using it. And that this is true, that the Romans did not have the staff, or, having it, they valued it little, you will read in all the engagements noted by Titus Livius in his history, where you will see that only very rarely is mention made of the shaft, rather he always says that, after hurling the spears, they put their hands on the sword. Therefore I want to leave this staff, and relate how much the Romans used the sword for offense, and for defense, the shield together with the other arms mentioned above.

The Greeks did not arm so heavily for defense as did the Romans, but in the offense relied more on this staff than on the sword, and especially the Phalanxes of Macedonia, who carried staffs which they called Sarisse, a good ten arms in length, with which they opened the ranks of the enemy and maintained order in the Phalanxes. And although other writers say they also had a shield, I do not know [for the reasons given above] how the Sarisse and the shield could exist together. In addition to this, in the engagement that Paulus Emilius had with Perseus, King of Macedonia, I do not remember mention being made of shields, but only of the Sarisse and the difficulty the Romans had in overcoming them. So that I conjecture that a Macedonian Phalanx was nothing else than a battalion of Swiss is today, who have all their strength and power in their pikes. The Romans [in addition to the arms] ornamented the infantry with plumes; which things make the sight of an army beautiful to friends, and terrible to the enemy. The arms for men on

horseback in the original ancient Roman (army) was a round
shield, and they had the head covered, but the rest (of the body)
without armor. They had a sword and a staff with an iron point,
long and thin; whence they were unable to hold the shield firm,
and only make weak movements with the staff, and because they
had no armor, they were exposed to wounds. Afterwards, with
time, they were armed like the infantry, but the shield was much
smaller and square, and the staff more solid and with two iron
tips, so that if the one side was encumbered, they could avail
themselves of the other. With these arms, both for the infantry
and the cavalry, my Romans occupied all the world, and it must
be believed, from the fruits that are observed, that they were
the best armed armies that ever existed.

And Titus Livius, in his histories, gives many proofs, where, in
coming to the comparison with enemy armies, he says, "but the
Romans were superior in virtue, kinds of arms, and discipline."
And, therefore, I have discussed more in particular the arms of
the victors than those of the losers. It appears proper to me to
discuss only the present methods of arming. The infantry have
for their defense a breastplate of iron, and for offense a lance
nine armlengths long, which they call a pike, and a sword at
their side, rather round in the point than sharp. This is the ordinary armament of the infantry today, for few have their arms
and shins (protected by) armor, no one the head; and those few
carry a halberd in place of a pike, the shaft of which [as you
know] is three armlengths long, and has the iron attached as an
axe. Among them they have three Scoppettieri (Exploders, i.e.,
Gunners), who, with a burst of fire fill that office which anciently was done by slingers and bow-men. This method of arming was established by the Germans, and especially by the Swiss,
who, being poor and wanting to live in freedom, were, and are,
obliged to combat with the ambitions of the Princes of
Germany, who were rich and could raise horses, which that people could not do because of poverty: whence it happened that
being on foot and wanting to defend themselves from enemies
who were on horseback, it behooved them to search the ancient
orders and find arms which should defend them from the fury
of horses. This necessity has caused them to maintain or redis-

cover the ancient orders, without which, as every prudent man affirms, the infantry is entirely useless. They therefore take up pikes as arms, which are most useful not only in sustaining (the attacks of) horses, but to overcome them. And because of the virtue of these arms and ancient orders, the Germans have assumed so much audacity, that fifteen or twenty thousand of them would assault any great number of horse, and there have been many examples of this seen in the last twenty five years. And this example of their virtue founded on these arms and these orders have been so powerful, that after King Charles passed into Italy, every nation has imitated them: so that the Spanish armies have come into a very great reputation.

Cosimo: What method of arms do you praise more, this German one or the ancient Roman?

Fabrizio: The Roman without any doubt, and I will tell you the good and the bad of one and the other. The German infantry can sustain and overcome the cavalry. They are more expeditious in marching and in organizing themselves, because they are not burdened with arms. On the other hand, they are exposed to blows from near and far because of being unarmed. They are useless in land battles and in every fight where there is stalwart resistance. But the Romans sustained and overcame the cavalry, as these (Germans) do. They were safe from blows near and far because they were covered with armor. They were better able to attack and sustain attacks having the shields. They could more actively in tight places avail themselves of the sword than these (Germans) with the pike; and even if the latter had the sword, being without a shield, they become, in such a case, (equally) useless. They (the Romans) could safely assault towns, having the body covered, and being able to cover it even better with the shield. So that they had no other inconvenience than the heaviness of the arms (armor) and the annoyance of having to carry them; which inconveniences they overcame by accustoming the body to hardships and inducing it to endure hard work. And you know we do not suffer from things to which we are accustomed. And you must understand this, that the infantry must be able to fight with infantry and cavalry, and those are always useless who cannot sustain the (attacks of the) cavalry, or if they are able to sustain them, nonetheless have fear of infantry who are better armed and organized than they. Now if you will consider the German and the Roman infantry, you will find in the German [as we have said] the aptitude of overcoming cavalry, but great disadvantages when fighting with an infantry organized as they are, and armed as the Roman. So that there will be this advantage of the one over the other, that the Romans could overcome both the infantry and the cavalry, and the Germans only the cavalry.

Cosimo: I would desire that you give some more particular example, so that we might understand it better.

Fabrizio: I say thusly, that in many places in our histories you will find the Roman infantry to have defeated numberless cavalry, but you will never find them to have been defeated by men on foot because of some defect they may have had in their arms or because of some advantage the enemy had in his. For if their manner of arming had been defective, it was necessary for them to follow one of two courses: either when they found one who was better armed than they, not to go on further with the conquest, or that they take up the manner of the foreigner, and leave off theirs: and since neither ensued, there follows, what can be easily conjectured, that this method of arming was better than that of anyone else. This has not yet occurred with the German infantry; for it has been seen that anytime they have had to combat with men on foot organized and as obstinate as they, they have made a bad showing; which results from the disadvantage they have in trying themselves against the arms of the enemy. When Filippo Visconti, Duke of Milan, was assaulted by eighteen thousand Swiss, he sent against them Count Carmignuola, who was his Captain at that time. This man with six thousand cavalry and a few infantry went to encounter them, and, coming hand to hand with them, was repulsed with very great damage. Whence Carmingnuola as a prudent man quickly recognized the power of the enemy arms, and how much they prevailed against cavalry, and the weakness of cavalry against those on foot so organized; and regrouping his forces, again went to meet the Swiss, and as they came near he made his men-at-arms descend from their horses, and in that manner fought with them, and killed all but three thousand, who, seeing themselves consumed without having any remedy, threw their arms on the ground and surrendered.

Cosimo: Whence arises such a disadvantage?

Fabrizio: I have told you a little while ago, but since you have not understood it, I will repeat it to you. The German infantry [as was said a little while ago] has almost no armor in defending itself, and use pikes and swords for offense. They come with these arms and order of battle to meet the enemy, who [if he is well equipped with armor to defend himself, as were the men-at-arms of Carmingnuola who made them descend to their feet] comes with his sword and order of battle to meet him, and he has no other difficulty than to come near the Swiss until he makes contact with them with the sword; for as soon as he makes contact with them, he combats them safely, for the Germans cannot use the pike against the enemy who is next to him because of the length of the staff, so he must use the sword, which is useless to him, as he has no armor and has to meet an enemy that is (protected) fully by armor. Whence, whoever considers the advantages and disadvantages of one and the other, will see that the one without armor has no remedy, but the one well armored will have no difficulty in overcoming the first blow and the first passes of the pike: for in battles, as you will understand better when I have demonstrated how they are put together, the men go so that of necessity they accost each other in a way that they are attacked on the breast, and if one is killed or thrown to the ground by the pike, those on foot who remain are so numerous that they are sufficient for victory. From this there resulted that Carmingnuola won with such a massacre of the Swiss, and with little loss to himself.

Cosimo: I see that those with Carmingnuola were men-at-arms, who, although they were on foot, were all covered with iron (armor), and, therefore, could make the attempt that they made; so that I think it would be necessary to arm the infantry in the same way if they want to make a similar attempt.

Fabrizio: If you had remembered how I said the Romans were armed, you would not think this way. For an infantryman who has his head covered with iron, his breast protected by a cuirass and a shield, his arms and legs with armor, is much more apt to defend himself from pikes, and enter among them, than is a man-at-arms (cavalryman) on foot. I want to give you a small modern example. The Spanish infantry had descended from Sicily into the Kingdom of Naples in order to go and meet Gonsalvo who was besieged in Barletta by the French. They came to an encounter against Monsignor D'Obigni with his men-at-arms, and with about four thousand German infantry. The Germans, coming hand to hand with their pikes low, pene- trated the (ranks of the) Spanish infantry; but the latter, aided by their spurs and the agility of their bodies, intermingled them- selves with the Germans, so that they (the Germans) could not get near them with their swords; whence resulted the death of almost all of them, and the victory of the Spaniards. Everyone knows how many German infantry were killed in the engage- ment at Ravenna, which resulted from the same causes, for the Spanish infantry got as close as the reach of their swords to the German infantry, and would have destroyed all of them, if the German infantry had not been succored by the French Cavalry: nonetheless, the Spaniards pressing together made themselves secure in that place. I conclude, therefore, that a good infantry not only is able to sustain the (attack) of cavalry, but does not have fear of infantry, which [as I have said many times] proceeds from its arms (armor) and organization (discipline).

Cosimo: Tell us, therefore, how you would arm them.

Fabrizio: I would take both the Roman arms and the German, and would want half to be armed as the Romans, and the other half as the Germans. For, if in six thousand infantry [as I shall explain a little later] I should have three thousand infantry with shields like the Romans, and two thousand pikes and a thousand gunners like the Germans, they would be enough for me; for I would place the pikes either in the front lines of the battle, or where I should fear the cavalry most; and of those with the shield and the sword, I would serve myself to back up the pikes and to win the engagement, as I will show you. So that I believe that an infantry so organized should surpass any other infantry today.

Cosimo: What you have said to us is enough as regards

infantry, but as to cavalry, we desire to learn which seems the more strongly armed to you, ours or that of the ancients?

Fabrizio: I believe in these times, with respect to saddles and stirrups not used by the ancients, one stays more securely on the horse than at that time. I believe we arm more securely: so that today one squadron of very heavily (armed) men-at-arms comes to be sustained with much more difficulty than was the ancient cavalry. With all of this, I judge, nonetheless, that no more account ought to be taken of the cavalry than was taken anciently; for [as has been said above] they have often in our times been subjected to disgrace by the infantry armed (armored) and organized as (described) above. Tigranus, King of Armenia, came against the Roman army of which Lucullus was Captain, with (an army) of one hundred fifty thousand cavalry, among whom were many armed as our men-at-arms, whom they called Catafratti, while on the other side the Romans did not total more than six thousand (cavalry) and fifteen thousand infantry; so that Tigranus, when he saw the army of the enemy, said: "These are just about enough horsemen for an embassy." nonetheless, when they came to battle, he was routed; and he who writes of that battle blames those Catafratti, showing them to be useless, because, he says, that having their faces covered, their vision was impaired and they were little adept at seeing and attacking the enemy, and as they were heavily burdened by the armor, they could not regain their feet when they fell, nor in any way make use of their persons. I say, therefore, that those People or Kingdoms which esteem the cavalry more than the infantry, are always weaker and more exposed to complete ruin, as has been observed in Italy in our times, which has been plundered, ruined, and overrun by foreigners, not for any other fault than because they had paid little attention to the foot soldiers and had mounted all their soldiers on horses. Cavalry ought to be used, but as a second and not the first reliance of an army; for they are necessary and most useful in undertaking reconnaissance, in overrunning and despoiling the enemy country, and to keep harassing and troubling the enemy army so as to keep it continually under arms, and to impede its provisions; but as to engagements and battles in the field, which are the important things in war and the object for which armies are organized, they are more useful in pursuing than in routing the enemy, and are much more inferior to the foot soldier in accomplishing the things necessary in accomplishing such (defeats).

Cosimo: But two doubts occur to me: the one, that I know that the Parthians did not engage in war except with cavalry, yet they divided the world with the Romans: the other, that I would like you to tell me how the (attack of) the cavalry can be sustained by the infantry, and whence arises the virtue of the latter and the weakness of the former?

Fabrizio: Either I have told you, or I meant to tell you, that my discussion on matters of war is not going beyond the limits of Europe. Since this is so, I am not obliged to give reasons for that which is the custom in Asia. Yet, I have this to say, that the army of Parthia was completely opposite to that of the Romans, as the Parthians fought entirely on horseback, and in the fighting were confused and disrupted, and their way of fighting was unstable and full of uncertainties. The Romans, it may be recalled, were almost all on foot, and fought pressed closely together, and at various times one won over the other, according as the site (of the battle) was open or tight; for in the latter the Romans were superior, but in the former the Parthians, who were able to make a great trial with that army with respect to the region they had to defend, which was very open with a seacoast a thousand miles distant, rivers two or three days (journey) apart from each other, towns likewise, and inhabitants rare: so that a Roman army, heavy and slow because of its arms and organization, could not pursue him without suffering great harm, because those who defended the country were on horses and very speedy, so that he would be in one place today, and tomorrow fifty miles distant. Because of this, the Parthians were able to prevail with cavalry alone, and thus resulted the ruin of the army of Crassus, and the dangers to those of Marcantonio. But [as I have said] I did not intend in this discussion of mine to speak of armies outside of Europe; and, therefore, I want to continue on those which the Romans and Greeks had organized in their time, and that the Germans do today.

But let us come to the other question of yours, in which you desire to know what organization or what natural virtue causes the infantry to be superior to the cavalry. And I tell you, first, that the horses cannot go in all the places that the infantry do, because it is necessary for them either to turn back after they have come forward, or turning back to go forward, or to move from a stand-still, or to stand still after moving, so that, without doubt, the cavalry cannot do precisely thus as the infantry. Horses cannot, after being put into disorder from some attack, return to the order (of the ranks) except with difficulty, and even if the attack does not occur; the infantry rarely do this. In addition to this, it often occurs that a courageous man is mounted on a base horse, and a base man on a courageous horse, whence it must happen that this difference in courage causes disorders. Nor should anyone wonder that a Knot (group) of infantry sustains every attack of the cavalry, for the horse is a sensible animal and knows the dangers, and goes in unwillingly. And if you would think about what forces make him (the horse) go forward and what keep him back, without doubt you will see that those which hold him back are greater than those which push him; for spurs make him go forward, and, on the other hand, the sword and the pike retain him. So that from both ancient and modern experiences, it has been seen that a small group of infantry can be very secure from, and even actually insuperable to, the cavalry. And if you should argue on this that the Elan with which he comes makes it more furious in hurling himself against whoever wants to sustain his attack, and he responds less to the pike than the spur, I say that, as soon as the horse so disposed begins to see himself at the point of being struck by the points of the pikes, either he will by himself check his gait, so that he will stop as soon as he sees himself about to be pricked by them, or, being pricked by them, he will turn to the right or left. If you want to make a test of this, try to run a horse against a wall, and rarely will you find one that will run into it, no matter with what Elan you attempt it. Caesar, when he had to combat the Swiss in Gaul, dismounted and made everyone dismount to their feet, and had the horses removed from the ranks, as they were more adept at fleeing than fighting.

But, notwithstanding these natural impediments that horses

have, the Captain who leads the infantry ought to select roads that have as many obstacles for horses as possible, and rarely will it happen that the men will not be able to provide for their safety from the kind of country. If one marches among hills, the location of the march should be such that you may be free from those attacks of which you may be apprehensive; and if you go on the plains, rarely will you find one that does not have crops or woods which will provide some safety for you, for every bush and embankment, even though small, breaks up that dash, and every cultivated area where there are vines and other trees impedes the horses. And if you come to an engagement, the same will happen to you as when marching, because every little impediment which the horse meets causes him to lose his fury. nonetheless, I do not want to forget to tell you one thing, that although the Romans esteemed much their own discipline and trusted very much on their arms (and armor), that if they had to select a place, either so rough to protect themselves from horses and where they could not be able to deploy their forces, or one where they had more to fear from the horses but where they were able to spread out, they would always take the latter and leave the former.

But, as it is time to pass on to the training (of the men), having armed this infantry according to the ancient and modern usage, we shall see what training they gave to the Romans before the infantry were led to battle. Although they were well selected and better armed, they were trained with the greatest attention, because without this training a soldier was never any good. This training consisted of three parts. The first, to harden the body and accustom it to endure hardships, to act faster, and more dexterously. Next, to teach the use of arms. The third, to teach the trainees the observance of orders in marching as well as fighting and encamping. These are the three principal actions which make an army: for if any army marches, encamps, and fights, in a regular and practical manner, the Captain retains his honor even though the engagement should not have a good ending. All the ancient Republics, therefore, provided such training, and both by custom and law, no part was left out. They therefore trained their youth so as to make them speedy in running, dextrous in jumping, strong in driving stakes and wrestling. And these three qualities are almost necessary in a soldier; for speed makes him adept at occupying places before the enemy, to come upon him unexpectedly, and to pursue him when he is routed. Dexterity makes him adept at avoiding blows, jumping a ditch, and climbing over an embankment. Strength makes him better to carry arms, hurl himself against an enemy, and sustain an attack. And above all, to make the body more inured to hardships, they accustom it to carry great weights. This accustoming is necessary, for in difficult expeditions it often happens that the soldier, in addition to his arms, must carry provisions for many days, and if he had not been accustomed to this hard work, he would not be able to do it, and, hence, he could neither flee from a danger nor acquire a victory with fame.

As to the teaching of the use of arms, they were trained in this way. They had the young men put on arms (armor) which weighed more than twice that of the real (regular) ones, and, as a sword, they gave them a leaded club which in comparison was very heavy. They made each one of them drive a pole into the ground so that three arm-lengths remained (above ground), and so firmly fixed that blows would not drive it to one side or have it fall to the ground; against this pole, the young men were trained with the shield and the club as against an enemy, and sometime they went against it as if they wanted to wound the head or the face, another time as if they wanted to puncture the flank, sometimes the legs, sometime they drew back, another time they went forward. And in this training, they had in mind making themselves adept at covering (protecting) themselves and wounding the enemy; and since the feigned arms were very heavy, the real ones afterwards seemed light. The Romans wanted their soldiers to wound (the enemy) by the driving of a point against him, rather than by cutting (slashing), as much because such a blow was more fatal and had less defense against it, as also because it left less uncovered (unprotected) those who were wounding, making him more adept at repeating his attack, than by slashing. Do you not wonder that those ancients should think of these minute details, for they reasoned that where men had to come hand to hand (in battle), every little advantage is of the greatest importance; and I will remind you of that, because the writers say of this that I have taught it to you. Nor did the ancients esteem it a more fortunate thing in a Republic than to have many of its men trained in arms; for it is not the splendor of jewels and gold that makes the enemy submit themselves to you, but only the fear of arms. Moreover, errors made in other things can sometimes be corrected afterwards, but those that are made in war, as the punishment happens immediately, cannot be corrected. In addition to this, knowing how to fight makes men more audacious, as no one fears to do the things which appear to him he has been taught to do. The ancients, therefore, wanted their citizens to train in every warlike activity; and even had them throw darts against the pole heavier than the actual ones: which exercise, in addition to making men expert in throwing, also makes the arm more limber and stronger. They also taught them how to draw the bow and the sling, and placed teachers in charge of doing all these things: so that when (men) were selected to go to war, they were already soldiers in spirit and disposition. Nor did these remain to teach them anything else than to go by the orders and maintain themselves in them whether marching or combatting: which they easily taught by mixing themselves with them, so that by knowing how to keep (obey) the orders, they could exist longer in the army.

Cosimo: Would you have them train this way now?

Fabrizio: Many of those which have been mentioned, like running, wrestling, making them jump, making them work hard under arms heavier than the ordinary, making them draw the crossbow and the sling; to which I would add the light gun, a new instrument [as you know], and a necessary one. And I would accustom all the youth of my State to this training: but that part of them whom I have enrolled to fight, I would (especially) train with greater industry and more solicitude, and I would train them always on their free days. I would also desire that they be taught to swim, which is a very useful thing, because there are not always bridges at rivers, nor ships ready: so that if your army does not know how to swim, it may be deprived of many advantages, and many opportunities to act well are taken away. The Romans, therefore, arranged that the young men be trained on the field of Mars, so that having the river Tiber nearby, they would be able after working hard in exercises on land to refresh themselves in the water, and also exercise them in their swimming.

I would also do as the ancients and train those who fight on horseback: which is very necessary, for in addition to knowing how to ride, they would know how to avail themselves of the horse (in maneuvering him). And, therefore, they arranged horses of wood on which they straddled, and jumped over them armed and unarmed without any help and without using their hands: which made possible that in a moment, and at a sign from the Captain, the cavalry to become as foot soldiers, and also at another sign, for them to be remounted. And as such exercises, both on foot and horseback, were easy at that time, so now it should not be difficult for that Republic or that Prince to put them in practice on their youth, as is seen from the experience of Western Cities, where these methods similar to these institutions are yet kept alive.

They divide all their inhabitants into several parts, and assign one kind of arms of those they use in war to each part. And as they used pikes, halberds, bows, and light guns, they called them pikemen, halberdiers, archers, and gunners. It therefore behooved all the inhabitants to declare in what order they wanted to be enrolled. And as all, whether because of age or other impediment, are not fit for war (combat), they make a selection from each order and they call them the Giurati (Sworn Ones), who, on their free days, are obliged to exercise themselves in those arms in which they are enrolled: and each one is assigned his place by the public where such exercises are to be carried on, and those who are of that order but are not sworn, participate by (contributing) money for those expenses which are necessary for such exercises. That which they do, therefore, we can do, but our little prudence does not allow us to take up any good proceeding.

From these exercises, it resulted that the ancients had good infantry, and that now those of the West have better infantry than ours, for the ancients exercised either at home as did those

Republics, or in the armies as did those Emperors, for the reasons mentioned above. But we do not want to exercise at home, and we cannot do so in the field because they are not our subjects and we cannot obligate them to other exercises than they themselves want. This reason has caused the armies to die out first, and then the institutions, so that the Kingdoms and the Republics, especially the Italian, exist in such a weak condition today.

But let us return to our subject, and pursuing this matter of training, I say, that it is not enough in undertaking good training to have hardened the men, made them strong, fast and dextrous, but it is also necessary to teach them to keep discipline, obey the signs, the sounds (of the bugle), and the voice of the Captain; to know when to stand, to retire, to go forward, and when to combat, to march, to maintain ranks; for without this discipline, despite every careful diligence observed and practiced, an army is never good. And without doubt, bold but undisciplined men are more weak than the timid but disciplined ones; for discipline drives away fear from men, lack of discipline makes the bold act foolishly. And so that you may better understand what will be mentioned below, you have to know that every nation has made its men train in the discipline of war, or rather its army as the principal part, which, if they have varied in name, they have varied little in the numbers of men involved, as all have comprised six to eight thousand men. This number was called a Legion by the Romans, a Phalanx by the Greeks, a Caterna by the Gauls. This same number, by the Swiss, who alone retain any of that ancient military umbrage, in our times is called in their language what in ours signifies a Battalion. It is true that each one is further subdivided into small Battaglia (Companies), and organized according to its purpose. It appears to me, therefore, more suitable to base our talk on this more notable name, and then according to the ancient and modern systems, arrange them as best as is possible. And as the Roman Legions were composed of five or six thousand men, in ten Cohorts, I want to divide our Battalion into ten Companies, and compose it of six thousand men on foot; and assign four hundred fifty men to each Company, of whom four hundred are heavily armed and fifty lightly armed: the heavily armed include three hundred with shields and swords, and will be called Scudati (shield bearers), and a hundred with pikes, and will be called pikemen: the lightly armed are fifty infantry armed with light guns, crossbows, halberds, and bucklers, and these, from an ancient name, are called regular (ordinary) Veliti: the whole ten Companies, therefore, come to three thousand shield bearers; a thousand ordinary pikemen, and one hundred fifty ordinary Veliti, all of whom comprise (a number of) four thousand five hundred infantry. And we said we wanted to make a Battalion of six thousand men; therefore it is necessary to add another one thousand five hundred infantry, of whom I would make a thousand with pikes, whom I will call extraordinary pikemen, (and five hundred lightly armed, whom I will call extraordinary Veliti): and thus my infantry would come [according as was said a little while ago] to be composed half of shield bearers and half among pikemen and other arms (carriers). In every Company, I would put in charge a Constable, four Centurions, and forty Heads of Ten, and in addition, a Head of the ordinary Veliti with five Heads of Ten. To the thousand extraordinary pikemen, I would assign three Constables, ten Centurions, and a hundred Heads of Ten: to the extraordinary Veliti, two Constables, five Centurions, and fifty Heads of Ten. I would also assign a general Head for the whole Battalion. I would want each Constable to have a distinct flag and (bugle) sound.

Summarizing, therefore, a Battalion would be composed of ten Companies, of three thousand shield bearers, a thousand ordinary pikemen, a thousand extraordinary pikemen, five hundred ordinary Veliti, and five hundred extraordinary Veliti: thus they would come to be six thousand infantry, among whom there would be one thousand five hundred Heads of Ten, and in addition fifteen Constables, with fifteen Buglers and fifteen flags, fifty five Centurions, ten Captains of ordinary Veliti, and one Captain for the whole Battalion with its flag and Bugler. And I have knowingly repeated this arrangement many times, so that then, when I show you the methods for organizing the Companies and the armies, you will not be confounded.

I say, therefore, that any King or Republic which would want to organize its subjects in arms, would provide them with these parties and these arms, and create as many battalions in the country as it is capable of doing: and if it had organized it according to the division mentioned above, and wanting to train it according to the orders, they need only to be trained Company by Company. And although the number of men in each of them could not by themselves provide a reasonably (sized) army, nonetheless, each man can learn to do what applies to him in particular, for two orders are observed in the armies: the one, what men ought to do in each Company: the other, what the Company ought to do afterwards when it is with others in an army: and those men who carry out the first, will easily observe the second: but without the first, one can never arrive at the discipline of the second. Each of these Companies, therefore, can by themselves learn to maintain (discipline in) their ranks in every kind and place of action, and then to know how to assemble, to know its (particular bugle) call, through which it is commanded in battle; to know how to recognize by it [as galleys do from the whistle] as to what they have to do, whether to stay put, or go forward, or turn back, or the time and place to use their arms. So that knowing how to maintain ranks well, so that neither the action nor the place disorganizes them, they understand well the commands of the leader by means of the (bugle) calls, and knowing how to reassemble quickly, these Companies then can easily [as I have said], when many have come together, learn to do what each body of them is obligated to do together with other Companies in operating as a reasonably (sized) army. And as such a general practice also is not to be esteemed little, all the Battalions can be brought together once or twice in the years of peace, and give them a form of a complete army, training it for several days as if it should engage in battle, placing the front lines, the flanks, and auxiliaries in their (proper) places.

And as a Captain arranges his army for the engagement either taking into account the enemy he sees, or for that which he does not see but is apprehensive of, the army ought to be trained for both contingencies, and instructed so that it can march and fight when the need arises; showing your soldiers how they should conduct themselves if they should be assaulted by this band or that. And when you instruct them to fight against an enemy they can see, show them how the battle is enkindled, where they have to retire without being repulsed, who has to take their places, what signs, what (bugle) calls, and what voice they should obey, and to practice them so with Companies and by mock attacks, that they have the desire for real battle. For a courageous army is not so because the men in it are courageous, but because the ranks are well disciplined; for if I am of the first line fighters, and being overcome, I know where I have to retire, and who is to take my place, I will always fight with courage seeing my succor nearby. If I am of the second line fighters, I would not be dismayed at the first line being pushed back and repulsed, for I would have presupposed it could happen, and I would have desired it in order to be he who, as it was not them, would give the victory to my patron. Such training is most necessary where a new army is created; and where the army is old (veteran), it is also necessary for, as the Romans show, although they knew the organization of their army from childhood, nonetheless, those Captains, before they came to an encounter with the enemy, continually exercised them in those disciplines. And Josephus in his history says, that the continual training of the Roman armies resulted in all the disturbance which usually goes on for gain in a camp, was of no effect in an engagement, because everyone knew how to obey orders and to fight by observing them. But in the armies of new men which you have to put together to combat at the time, or that you caused to be organized to combat in time, nothing is done without this training, as the Companies are different as in a complete army; for as much discipline is necessary, it must be taught with double the industry and effort to those who do not have it, and be maintained in those who have it, as is seen from the fact that many excellent Captains have tired themselves without any regard to themselves.

Cosimo: And it appears to me that this discussion has somewhat carried you away, for while you have not yet mentioned the means with which Companies are trained, you have discussed engagements and the complete army.

Fabrizio: You say the truth, and truly the reason is the affection I have for these orders, and the sorrow that I feel seeing that they are not put into action: nonetheless, have no fear, but I shall return to the subject. As I have told you, of first importance in the training of the Company is to know how to maintain ranks. To do this, it is necessary to exercise them in those orders, which they called Chiocciole (Spiralling). And as I told you that one of these Companies ought to consist of four hundred heavily armed infantry, I will stand on this number. They should, therefore, be arranged into eighty ranks (files), with five per file. Then continuing on either strongly or slowly, grouping them and dispersing them; which, when it is done, can be demonstrated better by deeds than by words: afterwards, it becomes less necessary, for anyone who is practiced in these exercises knows how this order proceeds, which is good for nothing else but to accustom the soldiers to maintain ranks. But let us come and put together one of those Companies.

I say that these can be formed in three ways: the first and most useful is to make it completely massive and give it the form of two squares: the second is to make the square with a homed front: the third is to make it with a space in the center, which they call Piazza (plaza). The method of putting together the first form can be in two steps. The first is to have the files doubled, that is, that the second file enters the first, the fourth into the third, and sixth into the fifth, and so on in succession; so that where there were eighty files and five (men) per file, they become forty files and ten per file. Then make them double another time in the same manner, placing one file within the other, and thus they become twenty files of twenty men per file. This makes almost a square, for although there are so many men on one side (of the square) as the other, nonetheless, on the side of the front, they come together so that (the side of) one man touches the next; but on the other side (of the square) the men are distant at least two arm lengths from each other, so that the square is longer from the front to the back (shoulders), then from one side (flank) to the other. (So that the rectangle thus formed is called two squares.)

And as we have to talk often today of the parts in front, in the rear, and on the side of this Company, and of the complete army, you will understand that when I will say either head or front, I mean to say the part in front; when I say shoulder, the part behind (rear); when I say flanks, the parts on the side.

The fifty ordinary Veliti of the company are not mixed in with the other files, but when the company is formed, they extend along its flanks.

The other method of putting together (forming) the company is this; and because it is better than the first, I want to place in front of your eyes in detail how it ought to be organized. I believe you remember the number of men and the heads which compose it, and with what arms it is armed. The form, there-fore, that this company ought to have is [as I have said] of twen-ty files, twenty men per file, five files of pikemen in front, and fifteen files of shield bearers on the shoulders (behind); two centurions are in front and two behind in the shoulders who have the office of those whom the ancients called Tergiduttori (Rear-leaders). The Constable, with the flag and bugler, is in that space which is between the five files of pikemen and the fif-teen of shield-bearers: there is one of the Captains of the Ten on every flank, so that each one is alongside his men, those who are on the left side of his right hand, those on the right side on his left hand. The fifty Veliti are on the flanks and shoulders (rear) of the company. If it is desired, now, that regular infantry be employed, this company is put together in this form, and it must organize itself thusly: Have the infantry be brought to eighty files, five per file, as we said a little while ago; leaving the Veliti at the head and on the tail (rear), even though they are outside this arrangement; and it ought to be so arranged that each Centurion has twenty files behind him on the shoulders, and those immediately behind every Centurion are five files of pike-men, and the remaining shield-bearers: the Constable, with his flag and bugler, is in that space that is between the pikemen and the shield-bearers of the second Centurion, and occupies the places of three shield-bearers: twenty of the Heads of Ten are on the Flanks of the first Centurion on the left hand, and twen-ty are on the flanks of the last Centurion on the right hand. And you have to understand, that the Head of Ten who has to guide (lead) the pikemen ought to have a pike, and those who guide the shield-bearers ought to have similar arms.

The files, therefore, being brought to this arrangement, and if it is desired, by marching, to bring them into the company to form the head (front), you have to cause the first Centurion to stop with the first file of twenty, and the second to continue to march; and turning to the right (hand) he goes along the flanks of the twenty stopped files, so that he comes head-to-head with the other Centurion, where he too stops; and the third Centurion continues to march, also turning to the right (hand), and marches along the flanks of the stopped file so that he comes head-to-head with the other two Centurions; and when he also stops, the other Centurion follows with his file, also going to the right along the flanks of the stopped file, so that he arrives at the head (front) with the others, and then he stops; and the two Centurions who are alone quickly depart from the front and go to the rear of the company, which becomes formed in that manner and with those orders to the point which we showed a little while ago. The Veliti extend themselves along its flanks, according as they were disposed in the first method; which method is called Doubling by the straight line, and this last (method) is called Doubling by the flanks.

The first method is easier, while this latter is better organized, and is more adaptable, and can be better controlled by you, for it must be carried out by the numbers, that from five you make ten, ten twenty, twenty forty: so that by doubling at your direction, you cannot make a front of fifteen, or twenty five or thirty or thirty five, but you must proceed to where the number is less. And yet, every day, it happens in particular situations, that you must make a front with six or eight hundred infantry, so that the doubling by the straight line will disarrange you: yet this (latter) method pleases me more, and what difficulty may exist, can be more easily overcome by the proper exercise and practice of it.

I say to you, therefore, that it is more important than anything to have soldiers who know how to form themselves quickly, and it is necessary in holding them in these Companies, to train them thoroughly, and have them proceed bravely forward or backward, to pass through difficult places without disturbing the order; for the soldiers who know how to do this well, are experienced soldiers, and although they may have never met the enemy face to face, they can be called seasoned soldiers; and, on the contrary, those who do not know how to maintain this order, even if they may have been in a thousand wars, ought always to be considered as new soldiers. This applies in forming them when they are marching in small files: but if they are formed, and then become broken because of some accident that results either from the location or from the enemy, to reorganize themselves immediately is the important and difficult thing, in which much training and practice is needed, and in which the ancients placed much emphasis. It is necessary, therefore, to do two things: first, to have many countersigns in the Company: the other, always to keep this arrangement, that the same infantry always remain in the same file. For instance, if one is commanded to be in the second (file), he will afterwards always stay there, and not only in this same file, but in the same position (in the file); it is to be observed [as I have said] how necessary are the great number of countersigns, so that, coming together with other companies, it may be recognized by its own men. Secondly, that the Constable and Centurion have tufts of feathers on their head-dress different and recognizable, and what is more important, to arrange that the Heads of Ten be recognized. To which the ancients paid very much attention, that nothing else would do, but that they wrote numbers on their bucklers, calling then the first, second, third, fourth, etc. And they were not above content with this, but each soldier had to write on his shield the number of his file, and the number of his place assigned him in that file. The men, therefore, being thus countersigned (assigned), and accustomed to stay within these limits, if they should be disorganized, it is easy to reorganize them all quickly, for the flag staying fixed, the Centurions and Heads of Ten can judge their place by eye, and bring the left from the right, or the right from the left, with the usual distances between; the infantry guided by their rules and by the difference in countersigns, can quickly take their proper places, just as, if you were the staves of a barrel which you had first countersigned, I would wager you would put it (the barrel) back together with great ease, but if you had not so countersigned them (the staves), it is impossible to reassemble (the barrel). This system, with diligence and practice, can be taught quickly, and can be quickly learned, and once learned is forgotten with difficulty; for new men are guided by the old, and in time, a province which has such training, would become entirely expert in war. It is also necessary to teach them to turn in step, and do so when he should turn from the flanks and by the soldiers in the front, or from the front to the flanks or shoulders (rear). This is very easy, for it is sufficient only that each man turns his body toward the side he is commanded to, and the direction in which they turned becomes the front. It is true that when they turn by the flank, the ranks which turn go outside their usual area, because there is a small space between the breast to the shoulder, while from one flank to the other there is much space, which is all contrary to the regular formation of the company. Hence, care should be used in employing it. But this is more important and where more practice is needed, is when a company wants to turn entirely, as if it was a solid body. Here, great care and practice must be employed, for if it is desired to turn to the left, for instance, it is necessary that the left wing be halted, and those who are closer to the halted one, march much slower then those who are in the right wing and have to run; otherwise everything would be in confusion.

But as it always happens when an army marches from place to place, that the companies not situated in front, not having to combat at the front, or at the flanks or shoulders (rear), have to move from the flank or shoulder quickly to the front, and when such companies in such cases have the space necessary as we indicated above, it is necessary that the pikemen they have on that flank become the front, and the Heads of the Ten, Centurions, and Constables belonging to it relocate to their proper places. Therefore, in wanting to do this, when forming them it is necessary to arrange the eighty files of five per file, placing all the pikemen in the first twenty files, and placing five of the Heads of Ten (of it) in the front of them and five in the rear: the other sixty files situated behind are all shield-bearers, who total to three hundred. It should therefore be so arranged, that the first and last file of every hundred of Heads of Ten; the Constable with his flag and bugler be in the middle of the first hundred (century) of shield-bearers; and the Centurions at the head of every century. Thus arranged, when you want the pike-men to be on the left flank, you have to double them, century by century, from the right flank: if you want them to be on the right flank, you have to double them from the left. And thus this company turns with the pikemen on the flank, with the Heads of Ten on the front and rear, with the Centurions at the front of them, and the Constable in the middle. Which formation holds when going forward; but when the enemy comes and the time for the (companies) to move from the flanks to the front, it can-not be done unless all the soldiers face toward the flank where the pikemen are, and then the company is turned with its files and heads in that manner that was described above; for the Centurions being on the outside, and all the men in their places, the Centurions quickly enter them (the ranks) without difficulty. But when they are marching frontwards, and have to combat in the rear, they must arrange the files so that, in forming the com-pany, the pikes are situated in the rear; and to do this, no other order has to be maintained except that where, in the formation of the company ordinarily every Century has five files of pike-men in front, it now has them behind, but in all the other parts, observe the order that I have mentioned.

Cosimo: You have said [if I remember well] that this method of training is to enable them to form these companies into an army, and that this training serves to enable them to be arranged within it. But if it should occur that these four hundred fifty infantry have to operate as a separate party, how would you arrange them?

Fabrizio: I will now guide you in judging where he wants to place the pikes, and who should carry them, which is not in any way contrary to the arrangement mentioned above, for although it may be the method that is observed when, together with other companies, it comes to an engagement, nonetheless, it is a rule that serves for all those methods, in which it should happen that you have to manage it. But in showing you the other two meth-ods for arranging the companies, proposed by me, I will also better satisfy your question; for either they are never used, or they are used when the company is above, and not in the company of others.

And to come to the method of forming it with two horns (wings), I say, that you ought to arrange the eighty files at five per file in this way: place a Centurion in the middle, and behind him twenty five files that have two pikemen (each) on the left side, and three shield-bearers on the right: and after the first five, in the next twenty, twenty Heads of Ten be placed, all between the pikemen and shield-bearers, except that those (Heads) who carry pikes stay with the pikemen. Behind these twenty five files thusly arranged, another Centurion is placed who has fifteen files of shield-bearers behind him. After these, the Constable between the flag and the bugler, who also has behind him another fifteen files of shield-bearers. The third Centurion is placed behind these, and he has twenty five files behind him, in each of which are three shield-bearers on the left side and two pikemen on the right: and after the first five files are twenty Heads of Ten placed between the pikemen and the shield-bearers. After these files, there is the fourth Centurion. If it is desired, therefore, to arrange these files to form a company with two horns (wings), the first Centurion has to be halted with the twenty five files which are behind him. The second Centurion then has to be moved with the fifteen shield-bearers who are on his rear, and turning to the right, and on the right flank of the twenty five files to proceed so far that he comes to the fifteen files, and here he halts. After, the Constable has to be moved with the fifteen files of shield bearers who are behind, and turning around toward the right, over by the right flank of the fifteen files which were moved first, marches so that he comes to their front, and here he halts. After, move the third Centurion with the twenty five files and with the fourth Centurion who is behind them, and turning to the right, march by the left flank of the last fifteen files of shield-bearers, and he does not halt until he is at the head of them, but continues marching up until the last files of twenty five are in line with the files behind. And, having done this, the Centurion who was Head of the first fifteen files of shield-bearers leaves the place where he was, and goes to the rear of the left angle. And thus he will turn a company of twenty five solid files, of twenty infantry per file, with two wings, on each side of his front, and there will remain a space between them, as much as would (be occupied by) ten men side by side. The Captain will be between the two wings, and a Centurion in each corner of the wing. There will be two files of pikemen and twenty Heads of Ten on each flank. These two wings (serve to) hold between them that artillery, whenever the company has any with it, and the carriages. The Veliti have to stay along the flanks beneath the pikemen. But, in wanting to bring this winged (formed) company into the form of the piazza (plaza), nothing else need be done than to take eight of the fifteen files of twenty per file and place them between the points of the two horns (wings), which then from wings become the rear (shoulder) of the piazza (plaza). The carriages are kept in this plaza, and the Captain and the flag there, but not the artillery, which is put either in the front or along the flanks. These are the methods which can be used by a company when it has to pass by suspicious places by itself. nonetheless, the solid company, without wings and without the plaza, is best. But in wanting to make safe the disarmed ones, that winged one is necessary.

The Swiss also have many forms of companies, among which they form one in the manner of a cross, as in the spaces between the arms, they keep their gunners safe from the attacks of the enemy. But since such companies are good in fighting by themselves, and my intention is to show how several companies united together combat with the enemy, I do not belabor myself further in describing it.

Cosimo: And it appears to me I have very well comprehended the method that ought to be employed in training the men in these companies, but [if I remember well] you said that in addition to the ten companies in a Battalion, you add a thousand extraordinary pikemen and four hundred extraordinary Veliti. Would you not describe how to train these?

Fabrizio: I would, and with the greatest diligence: and I would train the pikemen, group by group, at least in the formations of the companies, as the others; for I would serve myself of these more than of the ordinary companies, in all the particular actions, how to escort, to raid, and such things. But the Veliti I would train at home without bringing them together with the others, for as it is their office to combat brokenly (in the open, separately), it is not as necessary that they come together with the others or to train in common exercises, than to train them well in particular exercises. They ought, therefore, [as was said in the beginning, and now it appears to me laborious to repeat it] to train their own men in these companies so that they know how to maintain their ranks, know their places, return there quickly when either the evening or the location disrupts them; for when this is caused to be done, they can easily be taught the place the company has to hold and what its office should be in the armies. And if a Prince or a Republic works hard and puts diligence in these formations and in this training, it will always happen that there will be good soldiers in that country, and they will be superior to their neighbors, and will be those who give, and not receive, laws from other men. But [as I have told you] the disorder in which one exists, causes them to disregard and not to esteem these things, and, therefore, our training is not good: and even if there should be some heads or members naturally of virtue, they are unable to demonstrate it.

Cosimo: What carriages would you want each of these companies to have?

Fabrizio: The first thing I would want is that the Centurions or the Heads of Ten should not go on horseback: and if the Constables want to ride mounted, I would want them to have a mule and not a horse. I would permit them two carriages, and one to each Centurion, and two to every three Heads of Ten, for they would quarter so many in each encampment, as we will narrate in its proper place. So that each company would have thirty six carriages, which I would have (them) to carry the necessary tents, cooking utensils, hatchets, digging bars, sufficient to make the encampment, and after that anything else of convenience.

Cosimo: I believe that Heads assigned by you in each of the companies are necessary: nonetheless, I would be apprehensive that so many commanders would be confusing.

Fabrizio: They would be so if I would refer to one, but as I refer to many, they make for order; actually, without those (orders), it would be impossible to control them, for a wall which inclines on every side would need many and frequent supports, even if they are not so strong, but if few, they must be strong, for the virtue of only one, despite its spacing, can remedy any ruin. And so it must be that in the armies and among every ten men there is one of more life, of more heart, or at least of more authority, who with his courage, with words and by example keeps the others firm and disposed to fight. And these things mentioned by me, as the heads, the flags, the buglers, are necessary in an army, and it is seen that we have all these in our (present day) armies, but no one does his duty. First, the Heads of Ten, in desiring that those things be done because they are ordered, it is necessary [as I have said] for each of them to have his men separate, lodge with them, go into action with them, stay in the ranks with them, for when they are in their places, they are all of mind and temperament to maintain their ranks straight and firm, and it is impossible for them to become disrupted, or if they become disrupted, do not quickly reform their ranks. But today, they do not serve us for anything other than to give them more pay than the others, and to have them do some particular thing. The same happens with the flags, for they are kept rather to make a beautiful show, than for any military use. But the ancients served themselves of it as a guide and to reorganize themselves, for everyone, when the flag was standing firm, knew the place that he had to be near his flag, and always returned there. He also knew that if it were moving or standing still, he had to move or halt. It is necessary in an army, therefore, that there be many bodies, and that each body have its own flag and its own guide; for if they have this, it must be they have much courage and consequently, are livelier. The infantry, therefore, ought to march according to the flag, and the flag move according to the bugle (call), which call, if given well, commands the army, which proceeding in step with those, comes to serve the orders easily. Whence the ancients having whistles (pipes), fifes, and bugles, controlled (modulated) them perfectly; for, as he who dances proceeds in time with the music,

and keeping with it does not make a miss-step, so an army obedient in its movement to that call (sound), will not become disorganized. And, therefore, they varied the calls according as
they wanted to enkindle or quiet, or firm the spirits of men. And
as the sounds were various, so they named them variously. The
Doric call (sound) brought on constancy, Frigio, fury (boldness):
whence they tell, that Alexander being at table, and someone
sounding the Frigio call, it so excited his spirit that he took up
arms. It would be necessary to rediscover all these methods, and
if this is difficult, it ought not at least to be (totally) put aside by
those who teach the soldier to obey; which each one can vary
and arrange in his own way, so long as with practice he accus-
toms the ears of his soldiers to recognize them. But today, no
benefit is gotten from these sounds in great part, other than to
make noise.

Cosimo: I would desire to learn from you, if you have ever
pondered this with yourself, whence such baseness and disorganization arises, and such negligence of this training in our times?

Fabrizio: I will tell you willingly what I think. You know of
the men excellent in war there have been many famed in
Europe, few in Africa, and less in Asia. This results from (the
fact that) these last two parts of the world have had a
Principality or two, and few Republics; but Europe alone has
had some Kingdoms and an infinite number of Republics. And
men become excellent, and show their virtue, according as they
are employed and recognized by their Prince, Republic, or
King, whichever it may be. It happens, therefore, that where
there is much power, many valiant men spring up, where there
is little, few. In Asia, there are found Ninus, Cyrus, Artafersus,
Mithradates, and very few others to accompany these. In Africa,
there are noted [omitting those of ancient Egypt] Maximinius,
Jugurtha, and those Captains who were raised by the
Carthaginian Republic, and these are very few compared to
those of Europe; for in Europe there are excellent men without
number, and there would be many more, if there should be
named together with them those others who have been forgotten by the malignity of the time, since the world has been more
virtuous when there have been many States which have favored

virtue, either from necessity or from other human passion. Few men, therefore, spring up in Asia, because, as that province was entirely subject to one Kingdom, in which because of its greatness there was indolence for the most part, it could not give rise to excellent men in business (activity). The same happened in Africa: yet several, with respect to the Carthaginian Republic, did arise. More excellent men come out of Republics than from Kingdoms, because in the former virtue is honored much of the time, in the Kingdom it is feared; whence it results that in the former, men of virtue are raised, in the latter they are extinguished. Whoever, therefore, considers the part of Europe, will find it to have been full of Republics and Principalities, which from the fear one had of the other, were constrained to keep alive their military organizations, and honor those who greatly prevailed in them. For in Greece, in addition to the Kingdom of the Macedonians, there were many Republics, and many most excellent men arose in each of them. In Italy, there were the Romans, the Samnites, the Tuscans, the Cisalpine Gauls. France and Germany were full of Republics and Princes. Spain, the very same. And although in comparison with the Romans, very few others were noted, it resulted from the malignity of the writers, who pursued fortune and to whom it was often enough to honor the victors. For it is not reasonable that among the Samnites and Tuscans, who fought fifty years with the Roman People before they were defeated, many excellent men should not have sprung up. And so likewise in France and Spain. But that virtue which the writers do not commemorate in particular men, they commemorate generally in the peoples, in which they exalt to the stars (skies) the obstinacy which existed in them in defending their liberty. It is true, therefore, that where there are many Empires, more valiant men spring up, and it follows, of necessity, that those being extinguished, little by little, virtue is extinguished, as there is less reason which causes men to become virtuous. And as the Roman Empire afterwards kept growing, and having extinguished all the Republics and Principalities of Europe and Africa, and in greater part those of Asia, no other path to virtue was left, except Rome. Whence it resulted that men of virtue began to be few in Europe as in Asia, which virtue ultimately came to decline; for all the virtue being brought to Rome, and as it was corrupted, so almost the whole world came to be corrupted, and the Scythian people were able to come to plunder that Empire, which had extinguished the virtue of others, but did not know how to maintain its own. And although afterwards that Empire, because of the inundation of those barbarians, became divided into several parts, this virtue was not renewed: first, because a price is paid to recover institutions when they are spoiled; another, because the mode of living today, with regard to the Christian religion, does not impose that necessity to defend it that anciently existed, in which at the time men, defeated in war, were either put to death or remained slaves in perpetuity, where they led lives of misery: the conquered lands were either desolated or the inhabitants driven out, their goods taken away, and they were sent dispersed throughout the world, so that those overcome in war suffered every last misery. Men were terrified from the fear of this, and they kept their military exercises alive, and honored those who were excellent in them. But today, this fear in large part is lost, and few of the defeated are put to death, and no one is kept prisoner long, for they are easily liberated. The Citizens, although they should rebel a thousand times, are not destroyed, goods are left to their people, so that the greatest evil that is feared is a ransom; so that men do not want to subject themselves to dangers which they little fear. Afterwards, these provinces of Europe exist under very few Heads as compared to the past, for all of France obeys a King, all of Spain another, and Italy exists in a few parts; so that weak Cities defend themselves by allying themselves with the victors, and strong States, for the reasons mentioned, do not fear an ultimate ruin.

Cosimo: And in the last twenty five years, many towns have been seen to be pillaged, and lost their Kingdoms; which examples ought to teach others to live and reassume some of the ancient orders.

Fabrizio: That is what you say, but if you would note which towns are pillaged, you would not find them to be the Heads (Chief ones) of the States, but only members: as is seen in the sacking of Tortona and not Milan, Capua and not Naples,

Brescia and not Venice, Ravenna and not Rome. Which examples do not cause the present thinking which governs to change, rather it causes them to remain in that opinion of being able to recover themselves by ransom: and because of this, they do not want to subject themselves to the bother of military training, as it appears to them partly unnecessary, partly a tangle they do not understand. Those others who are slaves, to whom such examples ought to cause fear, do not have the power of remedying (their situation), and those Princes who have lost the State, are no longer in time, and those who have (the State) do not have (military training) or want it; for they want without any hardship to remain (in power) through fortune, not through their own virtue, and who see that, because there is so little virtue, fortune governs everything, and they want it to master them, not they master it. And that which I have discussed is true, consider Germany, in which, because there are many Principalities and Republics, there is much virtue, and all that is good in our present army, depends on the example of those people, who, being completely jealous of their State [as they fear servitude, which elsewhere is not feared] maintain and honor themselves all as Lords. I want this to suffice to have said in showing the reasons for the present business according to my opinion. I do not know if it appears the same to you, or if some other apprehension should have risen from this discussion.

Cosimo: None, rather I am most satisfied with everything. I desire above, returning to our principal subject, to learn from you how you would arrange the cavalry with these companies, and how many, how captained, and how armed.

Fabrizio: And it, perhaps, appears to you that I have omitted these, at which do not be surprised, for I speak little of them for two reasons: one, because this part of the army is less corrupt than that of the infantry, for it is not stronger than the ancient, it is on a par with it. However, a short while before, the method of training them has been mentioned. And as to arming them, I would arm them as is presently done, both as to the light cavalry as to the men-at-arms. But I would want the light cavalry to be all archers, with some light gunners among them, who, although of little use in other actions of war, are most useful in terrifying the peasants, and place them above a pass that is to be guarded by them, for one gunner causes more fear to them (the enemy) than twenty other armed men. And as to numbers, I say that departing from imitating the Roman army, I would have not less than three hundred effective cavalry for each battalion, of which I would want one hundred fifty to be men-at-arms, and a hundred fifty light cavalry; and I would give a leader to each of these parts, creating among them fifteen Heads of Ten per hand, and give each one a flag and a bugler. I would want that every ten men-at-arms have five carriages and every ten light cavalrymen two, which, like those of the infantry, should carry the tents, (cooking) utensils, hitches, poles, and in addition over the others, their tools. And do not think this is out of place seeing that men-at-arms have four horses at their service, and that such a practice is a corrupting one; for in Germany, it is seen that those men-at-arms are alone with their horses, and only every twenty have a cart which carries the necessary things behind them. The horsemen of the Romans were likewise alone: it is true that the Triari encamped near the cavalry and were obliged to render aid to it in the handling of the horses: this can easily be imitated by us, as will be shown in the distribution of quarters. That, therefore, which the Romans did, and that which the Germans do, we also can do; and in not doing it, we make a mistake. These cavalrymen, enrolled and organized together with a battalion, can often be assembled when the companies are assembled, and caused to make some semblance of attack among them, which should be done more so that they may be recognized among them than for any necessity. But I have said enough on this subject for now, and let us descend to forming an army which is able to offer battle to the enemy, and hope to win it; which is the end for which an army is organized, and so much study put into it.

THIRD BOOK

Cosimo: Since we are changing the discussion, I would like the questioner to be changed, so that I may not be held to be presumptuous, which I have always censured in others. I, therefore, resign the speakership, and I surrender it to any of these friends of mine who want it.

Zanobi: It would be most gracious of you to continue: but since you do not want to, you ought at least to tell us which of us should succeed in your place.

Cosimo: I would like to pass this burden on the Lord Fabrizio.

Fabrizio: I am content to accept it, and would like to follow the Venetian custom, that the youngest talks first; for this being an exercise for young men, I am persuaded that young men are more adept at reasoning, than they are quick to follow.

Cosimo: It therefore falls to you.

Luigi: And I am pleased with such a successor, as long as you are satisfied with such a questioner.

Fabrizio: I am certain that, in wanting to show how an army is well organized for undertaking an engagement, it would be necessary to narrate how the Greeks and the Romans arranged the ranks in their armies. nonetheless, as you yourselves are able to read and consider these things, through the medium of ancient writers, I shall omit many particulars, and will cite only those things that appear necessary for me to imitate, in the desire in our times to give some (part of) perfection to our army. This will be done, and, in time, I will show how an army is arranged for an engagement, how it faces a real battle, and how it can be trained in mock ones. The greatest mistake that those men make who arrange an army for an engagement, is to give it only one front, and commit it to only one onrush and one attempt (fortune). This results from having lost the method the ancients employed of receiving one rank into the other; for without this method, one cannot help the rank in front, or defend them, or change them by rotation in battle, which was practiced best by the Romans. In explaining this method, therefore, I want to tell how the Romans divided each Legion into three parts, namely, the Astati, the Princeps, and the Triari; of whom the Astati were placed in the first line of the army in solid and deep ranks, (and) behind them were the Princeps, but placed with their ranks more open: and behind these they placed the Triari, and with ranks so sparse, as to be able, if necessary, to receive the Princeps and the Astati between them. In addition to these, they had slingers, bow-men (archers), and other lightly armed, who were not in these ranks, but were situated at the head of the army between the cavalry and the infantry. These light armed men, therefore, enkindled the battle, and if they won [which rarely happened], they pursued the victory: if they were repulsed, they retired by way of the flanks of the army, or into the intervals (gaps) provided for such a result, and were led back among those who were not armed: after this proceeding, the Astati came hand to hand with the enemy, and who, if they saw themselves being overcome, retired little by little through the open spaces in the ranks of the Princeps, and, together with them, renewed the fight. If these also were forced back, they all retired into the thin lines of the Triari, and all together, en masse, recommenced the battle; and if these were defeated, there was no other remedy, as there was no way left to reform themselves. The cavalry were on the flanks of the army, placed like two wings on a body, and they sometimes fought on horseback, and sometimes helped the infantry, according as the need required. This method of reforming themselves three times is almost impossible to surpass, as it is necessary that fortune abandon you three times, and that the enemy has so much virtue that he overcomes you three times. The Greeks, with their Phalanxes, did not have this method of reforming themselves, and although these had many ranks and Leaders within them, nonetheless, they constituted one body, or rather, one front. So that in order to help one another, they did not retire from one rank into the other, as the Romans, but one man took the place of another, which they did in this way. Their Phalanxes were (made up) of ranks, and supposing they had placed fifty men per rank, when their front came against the enemy, only the first six ranks of all of them were able to fight, because their lances, which they called Sarisse, were so long, that the points of the lances of those in the sixth rank reached past the front rank. When they fought, therefore, if any of the first rank fell, either killed or wounded, whoever was behind him in the second rank immediately entered into his place, and whoever was behind him in the third rank immediately entered into the place in the second rank which had become vacant, and thus successively all at once the ranks behind restored the deficiencies of those in front, so that the ranks were always remained complete, and no position of the combatants was vacant except in the last rank, which became depleted because there was no one in its rear to restore it. So that the injuries which the first rank suffered, depleted the last, and the first rank always remained complete; and thus the Phalanxes, because of their arrangement, were able rather to become depleted than broken, since the large (size of its) body made it more immobile. The Romans, in the beginning, also employed Phalanxes, and instructed their Legions in a way similar to theirs. Afterwards, they were not satisfied with this arrangement, and divided the Legion into several bodies; that is, into Cohorts and Maniples; for they judged [as was said a little while ago] that that body should have more life in it (be more active) which should have more spirit, and that it should be composed of several parts, and each regulate itself.

The Battalions of the Swiss, in these times, employed all the methods of the Phalanxes, as much in the size and entirety of their organization, as in the method of helping one another, and when coming to an engagement they place the Battalions one on the flank of the other, or they place them one behind the other. They have no way in which the first rank, if it should retire, to be received by the second, but with this arrangement, in order to help one another, they place one Battalion in front and another behind it to the right, so that if the first has need of aid, the latter can go forward and succor it. They put a third Battalion behind these, but distant a gun shot. This they do, because if the other two are repulsed, this (third) one can make its way forward, and the others have room in which to retire, and avoid the onrush of the one which is going forward; for a large multitude cannot be received (in the same way) as a small body, and, therefore, the small and separate bodies that existed in a Roman Legion could be so placed together as to be able to receive one another among themselves, and help each other easily. And that this arrangement of the Swiss is not as good as that of the ancient Romans is demonstrated by the many examples of the Roman Legions when they engaged in battle with the Greek Phalanxes, and the latter were always destroyed by the former, because the kinds of arms [as I mentioned before] and this method of reforming themselves, was not able to maintain the solidity of the Phalanx. With these examples, therefore, if I had to organize an army, I would prefer to retain the arms and the methods, partly of the Greek Phalanxes, partly of the Roman Legions; and therefore I have mentioned wanting in a Battalion two thousand pikes, which are the arms of the Macedonian Phalanxes, and three thousand swords and shield, which are the arms of the Romans. I have divided the Battalion into ten Companies, as the Romans (divided) the Legion into ten Cohorts. I have organized the Veliti, that is the light armed, to enkindle the battle, as they (the Romans did). And thus, as the arms are mixed, being shared by both nations and as also the organizations are shared, I have arranged that each company have five ranks of pikes (pikemen) in front, and the remainder shields (swordsmen with shields), in order to be able with this front to resist the cavalry, and easily penetrate the enemy companies on foot, and the enemy at the first encounter would meet the pikes, which I would hope would suffice to resist him, and then the shields (swordsmen) would defeat him. And if you would note the virtue of this arrangement, you will see all these arms will execute their office completely. First, because pikes are useful against cavalry, and when they come against infantry, they do their duty well before the battle closes in, for when they are pressed, they become useless. Whence the Swiss, to avoid this disadvantage, after every three ranks of pikemen place one of halberds, which, while it is not enough, gives the pikemen room (to maneuver). Placing, therefore, our pikes in the front and the shields (swordsmen) behind, they manage to resist the cavalry, and in enkindling the battle, lay open and attack the infantry: but when the battle closes in, and they become useless, the shields and swords take their place, who are able to take care of themselves in every strait.

Luigi: We now await with desire to learn how you would arrange the army for battle with these arms and with these organizations.

Fabrizio: I do not now want to show you anything else other than this. You have to understand that in a regular Roman army, which they called a Consular Army, there were not more than two Legions of Roman Citizens, which consisted of six hundred cavalry and about eleven thousand infantry. They also had as many more infantry and cavalry which were sent to them by their friends and confederates, which they divided into two parts, and they called one the right wing, and the other the left wing, and they never permitted this (latter) infantry to exceed the number of the infantry of the Legion. They were well content that the cavalry should be greater in number. With this army which consisted of twenty two thousand infantry and about two thousand cavalry effectives, a Consul undertook every action and went on every enterprise. And when it was necessary to face a large force, they brought together two Consuls with two armies. You ought also to note that ordinarily in all three of the principal activities in which armies engage, that is, marching, camping, and fighting, they place the Legion in the middle, because they wanted that virtue in which they should trust most should be greater unity, as the discussion of all these three activities will show you. Those auxiliary infantry, because of the training they had with the infantry of the Legion, were as effective as the latter, as they were disciplined as they were, and therefore they arranged them in a similar way when organizing (for) an engagement. Whoever, therefore, knows how they deployed the entire (army). Therefore, having told you how they divided a Legion into three lines, and how one line would receive the other, I have come to tell you how the entire army was organized for an engagement.

If I would want, therefore, to arrange (an army for) an engagement in imitation of the Romans, just as they had two Legions, I would take two Battalions, and these having been deployed, the disposition of an entire Army would be known: for by adding more people, nothing else is accomplished than to enlarge the organization. I do not believe it is necessary that I remind you how many infantry there are in a Battalion, and that it has ten companies, and what Leaders there are per company, and what arms they have, and who are the ordinary (regular) pikemen and Veliti, and who the extraordinary, because a little while I distinctly told you, and I reminded you to commit it to memory as something necessary if you should want to understand all the other arrangements: and, therefore, I will come to the demonstration of the arrangement, without repeating these again. And it appears to me that ten Companies of a Battalion should be placed on the left flank, and the ten others of the other on the right. Those on the left should be arranged in this way. The five companies should be placed one alongside the other on the front, so that between one and the next there would be a space of four arm lengths which come to occupy an area of one hundred forty one arm lengths long, and forty wide. Behind these five Companies I would place three others, distant in a straight line from the first ones by forty arm lengths, two of which should come behind in a straight line at the ends of the five, and the other should occupy the space in the middle. Thus these three would come to occupy in length and width the same space as the five: but where the five would have a distance of four arm lengths between one another, this one would have thirty three. Behind these I would place the last two companies, also in a straight line behind the three, and distant from those three forty arm lengths, and I would place each of them behind the ends of the three, so that the space between them would be ninety one arm lengths. All of these companies arranged thusly would therefore cover (an area of) one hundred forty one arm lengths long and two hundred wide. The extraordinary pikemen I would extend along the flanks of these companies on the left side, distant twenty arm lengths from it, creating a hundred forty three files of seven per file, so that they should cover the entire length of the ten companies arranged as I have previously described; and there would remain forty files for protecting the wagons and the unarmed people in the tail of the army, (and) assigning the Heads of Ten and the Centurions in their (proper) places: and, of the three Constables, I would put one at the head, another in the middle, and the third in the last file, who should fill the office of Tergiduttore, as the ancients called the one placed in charge of the rear of the Army. But returning to the head (van) of the Army I say, that I would place the extraordinary Veliti alongside the extraordinary pikemen, which, as you know, are five hundred, and would place them at a distance of forty arm lengths. On the side of these, also on the left hand; I would place the men-at-arms, and would assign them a distance of a hundred fifty arm lengths away. Behind these, the light cavalry, to whom I would assign the same space as the men-at-arms. The ordinary Veliti I would leave around their companies, who would occupy those spaces which I placed between one company and another, who would act to minister to those (companies) unless I had already placed them under the extraordinary pikemen; which I would do or not do according as it should benefit my plans. The general Head of all the Battalions I would place in that space that exists between the first and second order of companies, or rather at the head, and in that space which exists between the last of the first five companies and the extraordinary pikemen, according as it should benefit my plans, surrounded by thirty or sixty picked men, (and) who should know how to execute a commission prudently, and stalwartly resist an attack, and should also be in the middle of the buglers and flag carriers. This is the order in which I would deploy a Battalion on the left side, which would be the deployment of half the Army, and would cover an area five hundred and eleven arm lengths long and as much as mentioned above in width, not including the space which that part of the extraordinary pikemen should occupy who act as a shield for the unarmed men, which would be about one hundred arm lengths. The other Battalions I would deploy on the right side exactly in the same way as I deployed those on the left, having a space of thirty arm lengths between our battalions and the other, in the head of which space I would place some artillery pieces, behind which would be the Captain general of the entire Army, who should have around him in addition to the buglers and flag carriers at least two hundred picked men, the greater portion on foot, among whom should be ten or more adept at executing every command, and should be so provided with arms and a horse as to be able to go on horseback or afoot as the need requires. Ten cannon of the artillery of the Army suffice for the reduction of towns, which should not exceed fifty pounds per charge, of which in the field I would employ more in the defense of the encampment than in waging a battle, and the other artillery should all be rather often than fifteen pounds per charge. This I would place in front of the entire army, unless the country should be such that I could situate it on the flank in a safe place, where it should not be able to be attacked by the enemy.

This formation of the Army thusly arranged, in combat, can maintain the order both of the Phalanxes and of the Roman Legions, because the pikemen are in front and all the infantry so arranged in ranks, that coming to battle with the enemy, and resisting him, they should be able to reform the first ranks from those behind according to the usage of the Phalanxes. On the other hand, if they are attacked so that they are compelled to break ranks and retire, they can enter into the spaces of the second company behind them, and uniting with them, (and) en masse be able to resist and combat the enemy again: and if this should not be enough, they can in the same way retire a second time, and combat a third time, so that in this arrangement, as to combatting, they can reform according to both the Greek method, and the Roman. As to the strength of the Army, it cannot be arranged any stronger, for both wings are amply provided with both leaders and arms, and no part is left weak except that part behind which is unarmed, and even that part has its flanks protected by the extraordinary pikemen. Nor can the enemy assault it in any part where he will not find them organized, and the part in the back cannot be assaulted, because there cannot be an enemy who has so much power that he can assail every side equally, for if there is one, you don't have to take the field with him. But if he should be a third greater than you, and as well organized as you, if he weakens himself by assaulting you in several places, as soon as you defeat one part, all will go badly for him. If his cavalry should be greater than yours, be most assured, for the ranks of pikemen that gird you will defend you from every onrush of theirs, even if your cavalry should be repulsed. In addition to this, the Heads are placed on the side so that they are able easily to command and obey. And the spaces that exist between one company and the next one, and between one rank and the next, not only serve to enable one to receive the other, but also to provide a place for the messengers who go and come by order of the Captain. And as I told you before, as the Romans had about twenty thousand men in an Army, so too ought this one have: and as other soldiers borrowed their mode of fighting and the formation of their Army from the Legions, so too those soldiers that you assembled into your two Battalions would have to borrow their formation and organization. Having given an example of these things, it is an easy matter to initiate it: for if the army is increased either by two Battalions, or by as many men as are contained in them, nothing else has to be done than to double the arrangements, and where ten companies are placed on the left side, twenty are now placed, either by increasing or extending the ranks, according as the place or the enemy should command you.

Luigi: Truly, (my) Lord, I have so imagined this army, that I see it now, and have a desire to see it facing us, and not for anything in the world would I desire you to become Fabius Maximus, having thoughts of holding the enemy at bay and delaying the engagement, for I would say worse of you, than the Roman people said of him.

Fabrizio: Do not be apprehensive. Do you not hear the artillery? Ours has already fired, but harmed the enemy little; and the extraordinary Veliti come forth from their places together with the light cavalry, and spread out, and with as much fury and the loudest shouts of which they are capable, assault the enemy, whose artillery has fired one time, and has passed over the heads of our infantry without doing them an injury. And as it is not able to fire a second time, our Veliti and cavalry have already seized it, and to defend it, the enemy has moved forward, so that neither that of friend or enemy can perform its office. You see with what virtue our men fight, and with what discipline they have become accustomed because of the training they have had, and from the confidence they have in the Army, which you see with their stride, and with the men-at-arms alongside, in marching order, going to rekindle the battle with the adversary. You see our artillery, which to make place for them, and to leave the space free, has retired to the place from which the Veliti went forth. You see the Captain who encourages them and points out to them certain victory. You see the Veliti and light cavalry have spread out and returned to the flanks of the Army, in order to see if they can cause any injury to the enemy from the flanks. Look, the armies are facing each other: watch with what virtue they have withstood the onrush of the enemy, and with what silence, and how the Captain commands the men-at-arms that they should resist and not attack, and do not detach themselves from the ranks of the infantry. You see how our light cavalry are gone to attack a band of enemy gunners who wanted to attack by the flank, and how the enemy cavalry have succored them, so that, caught between the cavalry of the one and the other, they cannot fire, and retire behind their companies. You see with what fury our pikemen attack them, and how the infantry is already so near each other that they can no longer manage their pikes: so that, according to the discipline taught by us, our pikemen retire little by little among the shields (swordsmen). Watch how in this (encounter), so great an enemy band of men-at-arms has pushed back our men-at-arms on the left side and how ours, according to discipline, have retired under the extraordinary pikemen, and having reformed the front with their aid, have repulsed the adversary, and killed a good part of them. In fact all the ordinary pikemen of the first company have hidden themselves among the ranks of the shields (swordsmen), and having left the battle to the swordsmen, who, look with what virtue, security, and leisure, kill the enemy. Do you not see that, when fighting, the ranks are so straitened, that they can handle the swords only with much effort? Look with what hurry the enemy moves; for, armed with the pike and their swords useless [the one because it is too long, the other because of finding the enemy too greatly armed], in part they fall dead or wounded, in part they flee. See them flee on the right side. They also flee on the left. Look, the victory is ours. Have we not won an engagement very happily? But it would have been won with greater felicity if I should have been allowed to put them in action. And see that it was not necessary to avail ourselves of either the second or third ranks, that our first line was sufficient to overcome them. In this part, I have nothing else to tell you, except to dissolve any doubts that should arise in you.

Luigi: You have won this engagement with so much fury, that I am astonished, and in fact so stupefied, that I do not believe I can well explain if there is any doubt left in my mind. Yet, trusting in your prudence, I will take courage to say that I intend. Tell me first, why did you not let your artillery fire more than one time? and why did you have them quickly retire within the army, nor afterward make any other mention of them? It seems to me also that you pointed the enemy artillery high, and arranged it so that it should be of much benefit to you. Yet, if it should occur [and I believe it happens often] that the lines are pierced, what remedy do you provide? And since I have commenced on artillery, I want to bring up all these questions so as not to have to discuss it any more. I have heard many disparage the arms and the organization of the ancient Armies, arguing that today they could do little, or rather how useless they would be against the fury of artillery, for these are superior to their arms and break the ranks, so that it appears to them to be madness to create an arrangement that cannot be held, and to endure hardship in carrying a weapon that cannot defend you.

Fabrizio: This question of yours has need [because it has so many items] of a long answer. It is true that I did not have the artillery fire more than one time, and because of it one remains in doubt. The reason is, that it is more important to one to guard

against being shot than shooting the enemy. You must understand that, if you do not want the artillery to injure you, it is necessary to stay where it cannot reach you, or to put yourself
behind a wall or embankment. Nothing else will stop it; but it is
necessary for them to be very strong. Those Captains who must
make an engagement cannot remain behind walls or embankments, nor can they remain where it may reach them. They
must, therefore, since they do not have a way of protecting
themselves, find one by which they are injured less; nor can they
do anything other than to undertake it quickly. The way of doing
this is to go find it quickly and directly, not slowly or en masse;
for, speed does not allow them to shoot again, and because the
men are scattered, they can injure only a few of them. A band of
organized men cannot do this, because if they march in a
straight line, they become disorganized, and if they scatter, they
do not give the enemy the hard work to rout them, for they have
routed themselves. And therefore I would organize the Army so
that it should be able to do both; for having placed a thousand
Veliti in its wings, I would arrange, that after our artillery had
fired, they should issue forth together with the light cavalry to
seize the enemy artillery. And therefore I did not have my
artillery fire again so as not to give the enemy time, for you cannot give me time and take it from others. And for that, the reason I did not have it fired a second time, was not to allow it to
be fired first; because, to render the enemy artillery useless,
there is no other remedy than to assault it; which, if the enemy
abandons it, you seize it; if they want to defend it, it is necessary
that they leave it behind, so that in the hands of the enemy or of
friends, it cannot be fired. I believe that, even without examples,
this discussion should be enough for you, yet, being able to give
you some from the ancients, I will do so. Ventidius, coming to
battle with the Parthians, the virtue of whom (the latter) in great
part consisted in their bows and darts, allowed them to come
almost under his encampments before he led the Army out,
which he only did in order to be able to seize them quickly and
not give them time to fire. Caesar in Gaul tells, that in coming
to battle with the enemy, he was assaulted by them with such
fury, that his men did not have time to draw their darts accord-

ing to the Roman custom. It is seen, therefore, that, being in the
field, if you do not want something fired from a distance to
injure you, there is no other remedy than to be able to seize it
as quickly as possible. Another reason also caused me to do
without firing the artillery, at which you may perhaps laugh, yet
I do not judge it to be disparaged. And there is nothing that
causes greater confusion in an Army than to obstruct its vision,
whence most stalwart Armies have been routed for having their
vision obstructed either by dust or by the sun. There is also
nothing that impedes the vision than the smoke which the
artillery makes when fired: I would think, therefore, that it
would be more prudent to let the enemy blind himself, than for
you to go blindly to find him. I would, therefore, not fire, or [as
this would not be approved because of the reputation the
artillery has] I would put it in the wings of the Army, so that firing it, its smoke should not blind the front of what is most
important of our forces. And that obstructing the vision of the
enemy is something useful, can be adduced from the example of
Epaminondas, who, to blind the enemy Army which was coming to engage him, had his light cavalry run in front of the enemy
so that they raised the dust high, and which obstructed their
vision, and gave him the victory in the engagement. As to it
appearing to you that I aimed the shots of artillery in my own
manner, making it pass over the heads of the infantry, I reply
that there are more times, and without comparison, that the
heavy artillery does not penetrate the infantry than it does,
because the infantry lies so low, and they (the artillery) are so
difficult to fire, that any little that you raise them, (causes) them
to pass over the heads of the infantry, and if you lower them,
they damage the ground, and the shot does not reach them (the
infantry). Also, the unevenness of the ground saves them, for
every little mound or height which exists between the infantry
and it (the artillery), impedes it. And as to cavalry, and especially
men-at-arms, because they are taller and can more easily be hit,
they can be kept in the rear (tail) of the Army until the time the
artillery has fired. It is true that often they injure the smaller
artillery and the gunners more than the latter (cavalry), to which
the best remedy is to come quickly to grips (hand to hand): and

if in the first assault some are killed [as some always do die] a good Captain and a good Army do not have to fear an injury that is confined, but a general one; and to imitate the Swiss, who never shun an engagement even if terrified by artillery, but rather they punish with the capital penalty those who because of fear of it either break ranks or by their person give the sign of fear. I made them [once it had been fired] to retire into the Army because it left the passage free to the companies. No other mention of it was made, as something useless, once the battle was started.

You have also said in regard to the fury of this instrument that many judge the arms and the systems of the ancients to be useless, and it appears from your talk that the moderns have found arms and systems which are useful against the artillery. If you know this, I would be pleased for you to show it to me, for up to now I do not know of any that have been observed, nor do I believe any can be found. So that I would like to learn from those men for what reasons the soldiers on foot of our times wear the breastplate or the corselet of iron, and those on horseback go completely covered with armor, since, condemning the ancient armor as useless with respect to artillery, they ought also to shun these. I would also like to learn for what reason the Swiss, in imitation of the ancient systems, for a close (pressed) company of six or eight thousand infantry, and for what reason all the others have imitated them, bringing the same dangers to this system because of the artillery as the others brought which had been imitated from antiquity. I believe that they would not know what to answer; but if you asked the soldiers who should have some experience, they would answer, first that they go armed because, even if that armor does not protect them from the artillery, it does every other injury inflicted by an enemy, and they would also answer that they go closely together as the Swiss in order to be better able to attack the infantry, resist the cavalry, and give the enemy more difficulty in routing them. So that it is observed that soldiers have to fear many other things besides the artillery, from which they defend themselves with armor and organization. From which it follows that as much as an Army is better armed, and as much as its ranks are more serrated and more powerful, so much more is it secure. So that whoever is of the opinion you mentioned must be either of little prudence, or has thought very little on this matter; for if we see the least part of the ancient way of arming in use today, which is the pike, and the least part of those systems, which are the battalions of the Swiss, which do us so much good, and lend so much power to our Armies, why shouldn't we believe that the other arms and other systems that they left us are also useful? Moreover, if we do not have any regard for the artillery when we place ourselves close together, like the Swiss, what other system than that can make us afraid? inasmuch as there is no other arrangement that can make us afraid than that of being pressed together. In addition to this, if the enemy artillery does not frighten me when I lay siege to a town, where he may injure me with great safety to himself, and where I am unable to capture it as it is defended from the walls, but can stop him only with time with my artillery, so that he is able to redouble his shots as he wishes, why do I have to be afraid of him in the field where I am able to seize him quickly? So that I conclude this, that the artillery, according to my opinion, does not impede anyone who is able to use the methods of the ancients, and demonstrate the ancient virtue. And if I had not talked another time with you concerning this instrument, I would extend myself further, but I want to return to what I have now said.

Luigi: We are able to have a very good understanding since you have so much discoursed about artillery, and in sum, it seems to me you have shown that the best remedy that one has against it when he is in the field and having an Army in an encounter, is to capture it quickly. Upon which, a doubt rises in me, for it seems to me the enemy can so locate it on a side of his army from which he can injure you, and would be so protected by the other sides, that it cannot be captured. You have [if you will remember] in your army's order for battle, created intervals of four arm lengths between one company and the next, and placed twenty of the extraordinary pikemen of the company there. If the enemy should organize his army similarly to yours, and place his artillery well within those intervals, I believe that from here he would be able to injure you with the greatest safety to himself, for it would not be possible to enter among the enemy forces to capture it.

Fabrizio: You doubt very prudently, and I will endeavor either to resolve the doubt, or to give you a remedy. I have told you that these companies either when going out or when fighting are continually in motion, and by nature always end up close together, so that if you make the intervals small, in which you would place the artillery, in a short time, they would be so closed up that the artillery can no longer perform its function: if you make them large to avoid this danger, you incur a greater, so that, because of those intervals, you not only give the enemy the opportunity to capture your artillery, but to rout you. But you have to know that it is impossible to keep the artillery between the ranks, especially those that are mounted on carriages, for the artillery travel in one direction, and are fired in the other, so that if they are desired to be fired while travelling, it is necessary before they are fired that they be turned, and when they are being turned they need so much space, that fifty carriages of artillery would disrupt every Army. It is necessary, therefore, to keep them outside the ranks where they can be operated in the manner which we showed you a short time ago. But let us suppose they can be kept there, and that a middle way can be found, and of a kind which, when closed together, should not impede the artillery, yet not be so open as to provide a path for the enemy, I say that this is easily remedied at the time of the encounter by creating intervals in your army which give a free path for its shots, and thus its fury will be useless. Which can be easily done, because the enemy, if it wants its artillery to be safe, must place it in the end portions of the intervals, so that its shots, if they should not harm its own men, must pass in a straight line, and always in the same line, and, therefore, by giving them room, can be easily avoided. Because this is a general rule, that you must give way to those things which cannot be resisted, as the ancients did to the elephants and chariots with sickles. I believe, rather I am more than certain, that it must appear to you that I prepared and won an engagement in my own manner; nonetheless, I will repeat this, if what I have said up to now is not enough, that it would be impossible for an

Army thus organized and armed not to overcome, at the first encounter, every other Army organized as modern Armies are organized, which often, unless they have shields (swordsmen), do not form a front, and are of an unarmed kind, which cannot defend themselves from a near-by enemy; and so organized that, if they place their companies on the flanks next to each other, not having a way of receiving one another, they cause it to be confused, and apt to be easily disturbed. And although they give their Armies three names, and divide them into three ranks, the Vanguard, the Company (main body) and the Rearguard, nonetheless, they do not serve for anything else than to distinguish them in marching and in their quarters: but in an engagement, they are all pledged to the first attack and fortune.

Luigi: I have also noted that in making your engagement, your cavalry was repulsed by the enemy cavalry, and that it retired among the extraordinary pikemen, whence it happened that with their aid, they withstood and repulsed the enemy in the rear. I believe the pikemen can withstand the cavalry, as you said, but not a large and strong Battalion, as the Swiss do, which, in your Army, have five ranks of pikemen at the head, and seven on the flank, so that I do not know how they are able to withstand them.

Fabrizio: Although I have told you that six ranks were employed in the Phalanxes of Macedonia at one time, nonetheless, you have to know that a Swiss Battalion, if it were composed of ten thousand tanks could not employ but four, or at most five, because the pikes are nine arm lengths long and an arm length and a half is occupied by the hands; whence only seven and a half arm lengths of the pike remain to the first rank. The second rank, in addition to what the hand occupies, uses up an arm's length of the space that exists between one rank and the next; so that not even six arm lengths of pike remain of use. For the same reasons, these remain four and one half arm lengths to the third rank, three to the fourth, and one and a half to the fifth. The other ranks are useless to inflict injury; but they serve to replace the first ranks, as we have said, and serve as reinforcements for those (first) five ranks. If, therefore, five of their ranks can control cavalry, why cannot five of ours control them, to whom five ranks behind them are also not lacking to sustain them, and give the same support, even though they do not have pikes as the others do? And if the ranks of extraordinary pikemen which are placed along the flanks seem thin to you, they can be formed into a square and placed by the flank of the two companies which I place in the last ranks of the army, from which place they would all together be able easily to help the van and the rear of the army, and lend aid to the cavalry according as their need may require.

Luigi: Would you always use this form of organization, when you would want to engage in battle?

Fabrizio: Not in every case, for you have to vary the formation of the army according to the fitness of the site, the kind and numbers of the enemy, which will be shown before this discussion is furnished with an example. But this formation that is given here, not so much because it is stronger than others, which is in truth very strong, as much because from it is obtained a rule and a system, to know how to recognize the manner of organization of the others; for every science has its generations, upon which, in good part, it is based. One thing only, I would remind you, that you never organize an army so that whoever fights in the van cannot be helped by those situated behind, because whoever makes this error renders useless the great part of the army, and if any virtue is eliminated, he cannot win.

Luigi: And on this part, some doubt has arisen in me. I have seen that in the disposition of the companies you form the front with five on each side, the center with three, and the rear with two; and I would believe that it should be better to arrange them oppositely, because I think that an army can be routed with more difficulty, for whoever should attack it, the more he should penetrate into it, so much harder would he find it: but the arrangement made by you appears to me results, that the more one enters into it, the more he finds it weak.

Fabrizio: If you would remember that the Triari, who were the third rank of the Roman Legions, were not assigned more than six hundred men, you would have less doubt, when you leave that they were placed in the last ranks, because you will

see that I (motivated by this example) have placed two companies in the last ranks, which comprise nine-hundred infantry; so
that I come to err rather with the Roman people in having taken
away too many, than few. And although this example should suffice, I want to tell you the reasons, which is this. The first front
(line) of the army is made solid and dense because it has to withstand the attack of the enemy, and does not have to receive any
friends into it, and because of this, it must abound in men, for
few men would make it weak both from their sparseness and
their numbers. But the second line, because it has to relieve the
friends from the first who have withstood the enemy, must have
large intervals, and therefore must have a smaller number than
the first; for if it should be of a greater or equal number, it would
result in not leaving any intervals, which would cause disorder,
or if some should be left, it would extend beyond the ends of
those in front, which would make the formation of the army
incomplete (imperfect). And what you say is not true, that the
more the enemy enters into the Battalions, the weaker he will
find them; for the enemy can never fight with the second line, if
the first one is not joined up with it: so that he will come to find
the center of the Battalion stronger and not weaker, having to
fight with the first and second (lines) together. The same thing
happens if the enemy should reach the third line, because here,
he will not only have to fight with two fresh companies, but with
the entire Battalion. And as this last part has to receive more
men, its spaces must be larger, and those who receive them lesser in number.

Luigi: And I like what you have said; but also answer me this.
If the five companies retire among the second three, and afterwards, the eight among the third two, does it not seem possible
that the eight come together then the ten together, are able to
crowd together, whether they are eight or ten, into the same
space which the five occupied.

Fabrizio: The first thing that I answer is, that it is not the
same space; for the five have four spaces between them, which
they occupy when retiring between one Battalion and the next,
and that which exists between the three or the two: there also
remains that space which exists between the companies and the

extraordinary pikemen, which spaces are all made large. There is added to this whatever other space the companies have when they are in the lines without being changed, for, when they are changed, the ranks are either compressed or enlarged. They become enlarged when they are so very much afraid, that they put themselves in flight: they become compressed when they become so afraid, that they seek to save themselves, not by flight, but by defense; so that in this case, they would compress themselves, and not spread out. There is added to this, that the five ranks of pikemen who are in front, once they have started the battle, have to retire among their companies in the rear (tail) of the army to make place for the shield-bearers (swordsmen) who are able to fight: and when they go into the tail of the army they can serve whoever the captain should judge should employ them well, whereas in the front, once the fight becomes mixed, they would be completely useless. And therefore, the arranged spaces come to be very capacious for the remaining forces. But even if these spaces should not suffice, the flanks on the side consist of men and not walls, who, when they give way and spread out, are able to create a space of such capacity, which should be sufficient to receive them.

Luigi: The ranks of the extraordinary pikemen, which you place on the flank of the army when the first company retires into the second, do you want them to remain firm, and become as two wings of the army or do you also want them to retire with the company. Which, if they have to do this, I do not see how they can, as they do not have companies behind them with wide intervals which would receive them.

Fabrizio: If the enemy does not fight them when he faces the companies to retire, they are able to remain firm in their ranks, and inflict injury on the enemy on the flank since the first companies had retired: but if they should also fight them, as seems reasonable, being so powerful as to be able to force the others to retire, they should cause them also to retire. Which they are very well able to do, even though they have no one behind who should receive them, for from the middle forward they are able to double on the right, one file entering into the other in the manner we discussed when we talked of the arrangement for doubling themselves. It is true, that when doubling, they should want to retire behind, other means must be found than that which I have shown you, since I told you that the second rank had to enter among the first, the fourth among the third, and so on little by little, and in this case, it would not be begun from the front, but from the rear, so that doubling the ranks, they should come to retire to the rear, and not to turn in front. But to reply to all of that, which (you have asked) concerning this engagement as shown by me, it should be repeated, (and) I again say that I have so organized this army, and will (again) explain this engagement to you for two reasons: one, to show you how it (the army) is organized: the other, to show you how it is trained. As to the systems, I believe you all most knowledgeable. As to the army, I tell you that it may often be put together in this form, for the Heads are taught to keep their companies in this order: and because it is the duty of each individual soldier to keep (well) the arrangement of each company, and it is the duty of each Head to keep (well) those in each part of the Army, and to know well how to obey the commands of the general Captain. They must know, therefore, how to join one company with another, and how to take their places instantly: and therefore, the banner of each company must have its number displayed openly, so that they may be commanded, and the Captain and the soldiers will more readily recognize that number. The Battalions ought also to be numbered, and have their number on their principal banner. One must know, therefore, what the number is of the Battalion placed on the left or right wing, the number of those placed in the front and the center, and so on for the others. I would want also that these numbers reflect the grades of positions in the Army. For instance, the first grade is the Head of Ten, the second is the head of fifty ordinary Veliti, the third the Centurion, the fourth the head of the first company, the fifth that of the second (company), the sixth of the third, and so on up to the tenth Company, which should be in the second place next to the general Captain of the Battalion; nor should anyone arrive to that Leadership, unless he had (first) risen through all these grades. And, as in addition to these Heads, there are the three Constables (in command) of the extraordinary pikemen, and the two of the extraordinary Veliti, I would want them to be of the grade of Constable of the first company, nor would I care if they were men of equal grade, as long as each of them should vie to be promoted to the second company. Each one of these Captains, therefore, knowing where his Company should be located, of necessity it will follow that, at the sound of the trumpet, once the Captain's flag was raised, all of the Army would be in its proper place. And this is the first exercise to which an Army ought to become accustomed, that is, to assemble itself quickly: and to do this, you must frequently each day arrange them and disarrange them.

Luigi: What signs would you want the flags of the Army to have, in addition to the number?

Fabrizio: I would want the one of the general Captain to have the emblem of the Army: all the others should also have the same emblem, but varying with the fields, or with the sign, as it should seem best to the Lord of the Army, but this matters little, so long as their effect results in their recognizing one another.

But let us pass on to another exercise in which an army ought to be trained, which is, to set it in motion, to march with a convenient step, and to see that, while in motion, it maintains order. The third exercise is, that they be taught to conduct themselves as they would afterwards in an engagement; to fire the artillery, and retire it; to have the extraordinary Veliti issue forth, and after a mock assault, have them retire; have the first company, as if they were being pressed, retire within the intervals of the second (company), and then both into the third, and from here each one return to its place; and so to accustom them in this exercise, that it become understood and familiar to everyone, which with practice and familiarity, will readily be learned. The fourth exercise is that they be taught to recognize commands of the Captain by virtue of his (bugle) calls and flags, as they will understand, without other command, the pronouncements made by voice. And as the importance of the commands depends on the (bugle) calls, I will tell you what sounds (calls) the ancients used. According as Thucydides affirms, whistles were used in the army of the Lacedemonians, for they judged that its pitch was more apt to make their Army proceed with seriousness and not with fury. Motivated by the same reason, the Carthaginians, in their first assault, used the zither. Alliatus, King of the Lydians, used the zither and whistles in war; but Alexander the Great and the Romans used horns and trumpets, like those who thought the courage of the soldiers could be increased by virtue of such instruments, and cause them to combat more bravely. But just as we have borrowed from the Greek and Roman methods in equipping our Army, so also in choosing sounds should we serve ourselves of the customs of both those nations. I would, therefore, place the trumpets next to the general Captain, as their sound is apt not only to inflame the Army, but to be heard over every noise more than any other sound. I would want that the other sounds existing around the Constables and Heads of companies to be (made by) small drums and whistles, sounded not as they are presently, but as they are customarily sounded at banquets. I would want, therefore, for the Captain to use the trumpets in indicating when they should stop or go forward or turn back, when they should fire the artillery, when to move the extraordinary Veliti, and by changes in these sounds (calls) point out to the Army all those moves that generally are pointed out; and those trumpets afterwards followed by drums. And, as training in these matters is of great importance, I would follow them very much in training your Army. As to the cavalry, I would want to use the same trumpets, but of lower volume and different pitch of sounds from those of the Captain. This is all that occurs to me concerning the organization and training of the Army.

Luigi: I beg you not to be so serious in clearing up another matter for me: why did you have the light cavalry and the extraordinary Veliti move with shouts and noise and fury when they attacked, but then in rejoining the Army you indicated the matter was accomplished with great silence: and as I do not understand the reason for this fact, I would desire you to clarify it for me.

Fabrizio: When coming to battle, there have been various opinions held by the ancient Captains, whether they ought either to accelerate the step (of the soldiers) by sounds, or have them go slowly in silence. This last manner serves to keep the ranks firmer and have them understand the commands of the Captain better: the first serves to encourage the men more. And, as I believe consideration ought to be given to both these methods, I made the former move with sound, and the latter in silence. And it does not seem to me that in any case the sounds are planned to be continuous, for they would impede the commands, which is a pernicious thing. Nor is it reasonable that the Romans, after the first assault, should follow with such sounds, for it is frequently seen in their histories that soldiers who were fleeing were stopped by the words and advice of the Captains, and changed the orders in various ways by their command: which would not have occurred if the sounds had overcome his voice.

FOURTH BOOK

Luigi: Since an engagement has been won so honorably under my Rule, I think it is well if I do not tempt fortune further, knowing how changeable and unstable it is. And, therefore, I desire to resign my speakership, and that, wanting to follow the order that belongs to the youngest, Zanobi now assume this office of questioning. And I know he will not refuse this honor, or we would rather say, this hard work, as much in order to (give) pleasure, as also because he is naturally more courageous than I: nor should he be afraid to enter into these labors, where he can thus be overcome, as he can overcome.

Zanobi: I intend to stay where you put me, even though I would more willingly stay to listen, because up to now I am more satisfied with your questions than those which occurred to me in listening to your discussions pleased me. But I believe it is well, Lords, that since you have time left, and have patience, we do not annoy you with these ceremonies of ours.

Fabrizio: Rather you give me pleasure, because this change of questioners makes me know the various geniuses, and your various desires. Is there anything remaining of the matter discussed which you think should be added?

Zanobi: There are two things I desire before we pass on to another part: the one is, that you would show me if there is another form of organizing the Army which may occur to you: the other, what considerations ought a Captain have before going to battle, and if some accident should arise concerning it, what remedies can be made.

Fabrizio: I will make an effort to satisfy you, I will not reply to your questions in detail; for, when I answer one, often it will also answer another. I have told you that I proposed a form for the Army which should fill all the requirements according to the (nature of) the enemy and the site, because in this case, one proceeds according to the site and the enemy. But note this, that there is no greater peril than to over extend the front of your army, unless you have a very large and very brave Army: otherwise you have to make it rather wide and of short length, than of long length and very narrow. For when you have a small force compared to the enemy, you ought to seek other remedies; for example, arrange your army so that you are girded on a side by rivers or swamps, so that you cannot be surrounded or gird yourself on the flanks with ditches, as Caesar did in Gaul. In this case, you have to take the flexibility of being able to enlarge or compress your front, according to the numbers of the enemy: and if the enemy is of a lesser number, you ought to seek wide places, especially if you have your forces so disciplined, that you are able not only to surround the enemy, but extend your ranks, because in rough and difficult places, you do not have the advantage of being able to avail yourself of (all) your ranks. Hence it happened that the Romans almost always sought open fields, and avoided the difficult ones. On the other hand [as I have said] you ought to, if you have either a small force or a poorly disciplined one, for you have to seek places where a small number can defend you, or where inexperience may not cause you injury. Also, higher places ought to be sought so as to be able more easily to attack (the enemy). nonetheless, one ought to be aware not to arrange your Army on a beach and in a place near the adjoining hills, where the enemy Army can come; because in this case, with respect to the artillery, the higher place would be disadvantageous to you, because you could continuously and conveniently be harmed by the enemy artillery, without being able to undertake any remedy, and similarly, impeded by your own men, you cannot conveniently injure him. Whoever organizes an Army for battle, ought also to have regard for both the sun and the wind, that the one and the other do not strike the front, because both impede your vision, the one with its rays, the other with dust. And in addition, the wind does not aid the arms that are thrown at the enemy, and makes their blows more feeble. And as to the sun, it is not enough that you take care that it is not in your face at the time, but you must think about it not harming you when it comes up. And because of this, in arranging the army, I would have it (the sun) behind them, so that much time should pass before it should come in front of you. This method was observed by Hannibal at Cannae and by Marius against the Cimbrians. If you should be greatly inferior in cavalry, arrange your army between vines and trees, and such impediments, as the Spaniards did in our times when they routed the French in the Kingdom (of Naples) on the Cirignuola. And it has been frequently seen that the same soldiers, when they changed only their arrangement and the location, from being overcome became victorious, as happened to the Carthaginians, who, after having been often defeated by Marius Regulus, were afterwards victorious, through the counsel of Xantippe, the Lacedemonian, who had them descend to the plain, where, by the virtue of their cavalry and Elephants, they were able to overcome the Romans. And it appears to me, according to the examples of the ancients, that almost all the excellent Captains, when they learned that the enemy had strengthened one side of the company, did not attack the stronger side, but the weaker, and the other stronger side they opposed to the weaker: then, when starting a battle, they cornered the stronger part that it only resist the enemy, and not push it back, and the weaker part that it allow itself to be overcome, and retire into the rear ranks of the Army. This causes two great disorders to the enemy: the first, that he finds his strongest part surrounded: the second is, that as it appears to them they will obtain the victory quickly, it rarely happens that he will not become disorganized, whence his defeat quickly results. Cornelius Scipio, when he was in Spain, (fighting) against Hasdrubal, the Carthaginian, and knowing that Hasdrubal was noted, that in arranging the Army, placed his legions in the center, which constituted the strongest part of his Army, and therefore, when Hasdrubal was to proceed in this manner, afterwards, when he came to the engagement, changed the arrangement, and put his Legions in the wings of the Army,

and placed his weakest forces in the center. Then when they
came hand to hand, he quickly had those forces in the center to
walk slowly, and the wings to move forward swiftly: so that only
the wings of both armies fought, and the ranks in the center,
being distant from each other, did not join (in battle), and thus
the strongest part of (the army of) Scipio came to fight the
weakest part of (that of) Hasdrubal, and defeated it. This
method at that time was useful, but today, because of the
artillery, could not be employed, because that space that existed
between one and the other army, gives them time to fire, which
is most pernicious, as we said above. This method, therefore,
must be set aside, and be used, as was said a short time ago,
when all the Army is engaged, and the weaker part made to
yield.

When a Captain finds himself to have an army larger than
that of the enemy, and not wanting to be prevented from surrounding him, arranges his Army with fronts equal to those of
the enemy: then when the battle is started, has his front retire
and the flanks extend little by little, and it will always happen
that the enemy will find himself surrounded without being
aware of it. When a Captain wants to fight almost secure in not
being routed, he arranges his army in a place where he has a safe
refuge nearby, either amid swamps or mountains or in a powerful city; for, in this manner, he cannot be pursued by the enemy,
but the enemy cannot be pursued by him. This means was
employed by Hannibal when fortune began to become adverse
for him, and he was apprehensive of the valor of Marcus
Marcellus. Several, in order to disorganize the ranks of the
enemy, have commanded those who are lightly armed, that they
begin the fight, and having begun it, retire among the ranks; and
when the Armies afterwards have joined fronts together, and
each front is occupied in fighting, they have allowed them to
issue forth from the flanks of the companies, and disorganized
and routed them. If anyone finds himself inferior in cavalry, he
can, in addition to the methods mentioned, place a company of
pikemen behind his cavalry, and in the fighting, arrange for
them to give way for the pikemen, and he will always remain
superior. Many have accustomed some of the lightly armed

infantry to get used to combat amidst the cavalry, and this has been a very great help to the cavalry. Of all those who have organized Armies for battle, the most praiseworthy have been Hannibal and Scipio when they were fighting in Africa: and as Hannibal had his Army composed of Carthaginians and auxiliaries of various kinds, he placed eighty Elephants in the first van, then placed the auxiliaries, after these he placed his Carthaginians, and in the rear, he placed the Italians, whom he trusted little. He arranged matters thusly, because the auxiliaries, having the enemy in front and their rear closed by his men, they could not flee: so that being compelled to fight, they should overcome or tire out the Romans, thinking afterwards with his forces of virtue, fresh, he could easily overcome the already tired Romans. In the encounter with this arrangement, Scipio placed the Astati, the Principi, and the Triari, in the accustomed fashion for one to be able to receive the other, and one to help the other. He made the vans of the army full of intervals; and so that they should not be seen through, but rather appear united, he filled them with Veliti, whom he commanded that, as soon as the Elephants arrived, they should give way, and enter through the regular spaces among the legions, and leave the way open to the Elephants: and thus come to render their attack vain, so that coming hand to hand with them, he was superior.

Zanobi: You have made me remember in telling me of this engagement, that Scipio, during the fight, did not have the Astati retire into the ranks of the Principi, but divided them and had them retire into the wings of the army, so as to make room for the Principi, if he wanted to push them forward. I would desire, therefore, that you tell me what reason motivated him not to observe the accustomed arrangement.

Fabrizio: I will tell you. Hannibal had placed all the virtue of his army in the second line; whence Scipio, in order to oppose a similar virtue to it, assembled the Principi and the Triari; so that the intervals of the Principi being occupied by the Triari, there was no place to receive the Astati, and therefore, he caused the Astati to be divided and enter the wings of the army, and did not bring them among the Principi. But take note that this method of opening up the first lines to make a place for the second, cannot be employed except when the other are superior, because then the convenience exists to be able to do it, as Scipio was able to. But being inferior and repulsed, it cannot be done except with your manifest ruin: and, therefore, you must have ranks in the rear which will receive you. But let us return to our discussion. The ancient Asiatics [among other things thought up by them to injure the enemy] used chariots which had scythes on their sides, so that they not only served to open up the lines with their attack, but also kill the adversary with the scythes. Provisions against these attacks were made in three ways. It was resisted by the density of the ranks, or they were received within the lines as were the Elephants, or a stalwart resistance was made with some stratagems, as did Sulla, the Roman, against Archelaus, who had many of those chariots which they called Falcati; he (Sulla), in order to resist them, fixed many poles in the ground behind the first ranks, by which the chariots, being resisted, lost their impetus. And note is to be taken of the new method which Sulla used against this man in arranging the army, since he put the Veliti and the cavalry in the rear, and all the heavily armed in front, leaving many intervals in order to be able to send those in the rear forward if necessity should require it; whence when the battle was started, with the aid of the cavalry, to whom he gave the way, he obtained the victory. To want to worry the enemy during the battle, something must be made to happen which dismays him, either by announcing new help which is arriving, or by showing things which look like it, so that the enemy, being deceived by that sight, becomes frightened; and when he is frightened, can be easily overcome. These methods were used by the Roman Consuls Minucius Rufus and Accilius Glabrius. Caius Sulpicius also placed many soldier-packs on mules and other animals useless in war, but in a manner that they looked like men-at-arms, and commanded that they appear on a hill while they were (in) hand to hand (combat) with the Gauls: whence his victory resulted. Marius did the same when he was fighting against the Germans. Feigned assaults, therefore, being of great value while the battle lasts, it happens that many are benefited by the real (assaults), especially if, improvised in the middle of the battle, it is able to attack the enemy from behind or on the sides. Which can be done only with difficulty, unless the (nature of the) country helps you; for if it is open, part of your forces cannot be speeded, as must be done in such enterprises: but in wooded or mountainous places, and hence capable of ambush, part of your forces can be well hidden, so that the enemy may be assaulted, suddenly and without his expecting it, which will always be the cause of giving you the victory. And sometimes it has been very important, while the battle goes on, to plant voices which announce the killed of the enemy Captain, or to have defeated some other part of the army; and this often has given the victory to whoever used it. The enemy cavalry may be easily disturbed by unusual forms (sights) or noises; as did Croesus, who opposed camels to the cavalry of his adversaries, and Pyrrhus who opposed elephants to the Roman cavalry, the sight of which disturbed and disorganized it. In our times, the Turk routed the Shah in Persia and the Soldan in Syria with nothing else than the noise of guns, which so affected their cavalry by their unaccustomed noises, that the Turk was able easily to defeat it. The Spaniards, to overcome the army of Hamilcar, placed in their first lines chariots full of tow drawn by oxen, and when they had come to battle, set fire to them, whence the oxen, wanting to flee the fire, hurled themselves on the army of Hamilcar and dispersed it. As we mentioned, where the country is suitable, it is usual to deceive the enemy when in combat by drawing him into ambushes: but when it is open and spacious, many have employed the making (digging) of ditches, and then covering them lightly with earth and branches, but leaving several places (spaces) solid in order to be able to retire between them; then when the battle is started, retire through them, and the enemy pursuing, comes to ruin in them. If, during the battle, some accident befalls you which dismays your soldiers, it is a most prudent thing to know how to dissimulate and divert them to (something) good, as did Lucius Sulla, who, while the fighting was going on, seeing that a great part of his forces had gone over to the side of the enemy, and that this had dismayed his men, quickly caused it to be understood throughout the entire army that everything was happening by his order, and this not only did not disturb the army, but so increased its courage that it was victorious. It also happened to Sulla, that having sent certain soldiers to undertake certain business, and they having been killed, in order that his army would not be dismayed said, that because he had found them unfaithful, he had cunningly sent them into the hands of the enemy. Sertorious, when undertaking an engagement in Spain, killed one who had pointed out to him the slaying of one of his Heads, for fear that by telling the same to the others, he should dismay them. It is a difficult matter to stop an army already in flight, and return it to battle. And you have to make this distinction: either they are entirely in flight (motion), and here it is impossible to return them: or only a part are in flight, and here there is some remedy. Many Roman Captains, by getting in front of those fleeing, have stopped them, by making them ashamed of their flight, as did Lucius Sulla, who, when a part of his Legions had already turned, driven by the forces of Mithradates, with his sword in hand he got in front of them and shouted, "if anyone asks you where you have left your Captain, tell them, we have left him in Boetia fighting." The Consul Attilius opposed those who fled with those who did not flee, and made them understand that if they did not turn about, they would be killed by both friends and enemies. Phillip of Macedonia, when he learned that his men were afraid of the Scythian soldiers, put some of his most trusted cavalry behind his army, and commissioned them to kill anyone who fled; whence his men, preferring to die fighting rather than in flight, won. Many Romans, not so much in order to stop a flight, as to give their men an occasion to exhibit greater prowess, while they were fighting, have taken a banner out of their hands, and tossing it amid the enemy, offered rewards to whoever would recover it.

I do not believe it is out of order to add to this discussion those things that happen after a battle, especially as they are brief, and not to be omitted, and conform greatly to this discussion. I will tell you, therefore, how engagements are lost, or are won. When one wins, he ought to follow up the victory with all speed, and imitate Caesar in this case, and not Hannibal, who, because he had stopped after he had defeated the Romans at Cannae, lost the Empire of Rome. The other (Caesar) never rested after a victory, but pursued the routed enemy with great impetus and fury, until he had completely assaulted it. But when one loses, a Captain ought to see if something useful to him can result from this loss, especially if some residue of the army remains to him. An opportunity can arise from the unawareness of the enemy, which frequently becomes obscured after a victory, and gives you the occasion to attack him; as Martius, the Roman, attacked the Carthaginian army, which, having killed the two Scipios and defeated their armies, thought little of that remnant of the forces who, with Martius, remained alive; and was (in turn) attacked and routed by him. It is seen, therefore, that there is nothing so capable of success as that which the enemy believes you cannot attempt, because men are often injured more when they are less apprehensive. A Captain ought, therefore, when he cannot do this, at least endeavor with industry to restrict the injury caused by the defeat. And to do this, it is necessary for you to take steps that the enemy is not able to follow you easily, or give him cause for delay. In the first case some, after they realize they are losing, order their Leaders to flee in several parts by different paths, having (first) given an order where they should afterward reassemble, so that the enemy, fearing to divide his forces, would leave all or a greater part of them safe. In the second case, many have thrown down their most precious possessions in front of the enemy, so that being retarded by plundering, he gave them more time for flight. Titus Dimius used not a little astuteness in hiding the injury received in battle; for, after he had fought until nightfall with a loss of many of his men, caused a good many of them to be buried during the night; whence in the morning, the enemy seeing so many of their dead and so few Romans, believing they had had the disadvantage, fled. I believe I have thus confused you, as I said, (but) satisfied your question in good part: it is true, that concerning the shape of the army, there remains for me to tell you how sometimes it is customary for some Captains to make the front in the form of a wedge, judging in that way to be able more readily to open (penetrate) the Army of the enemy. In opposition to this shape they customarily would use a form of a scissor, so as to be able to receive that wedge into that space, and surround and fight it from every side. On this, I would like you to have this general rule, that the greatest remedy used against the design of the enemy, is to do that willingly which he designs for you to do by force, because doing it willingly you do it with order and to your advantage, but to his disadvantage: if you should do it by force, it would be to your ruin. As to the fortifying of this, I would not care to repeat anything already said. Does the adversary make a wedge in order to open your ranks? If you proceed with yours open, you disorganize him, and he does not disorganize you. Hannibal placed Elephants in front of his Army to open that of the Army of Scipio; Scipio went with his open and was the cause of his own victory and the ruin of the former (Hannibal). Hasdrubal placed his most stalwart forces in the center of the van of his Army to push back the forces of Scipio: Scipio commanded in like fashion that they should retire, and defeated him. So that such plans, when they are put forward, are the cause for the victory of him against whom they were organized.

It remains for me yet, if I remember well, to tell you what considerations a Captain ought to take into account before going into battle: upon which I have to tell you first that a Captain never has to make an engagement, if he does not have the advantage, or if he is not compelled to. Advantages arise from the location, from the organization, and from having either greater or better forces. Necessity, (compulsion) arises when you see that, by not fighting, you must lose in an event; for example, when you see you are about to lack money, and therefore your Army has to be dissolved in any case; when hunger is about to assail you, or when you expect the enemy to be reinforced again by new forces. In these cases, one ought always to fight, even at your disadvantage; for it is much better to try your fortune when it can favor you, than by not trying, see your ruin sure: and in such a case, it is as serious an error for a Captain not to fight, as it is to pass up an opportunity to win, either from ignorance, or from cowardice. The enemy sometimes gives you the advantage, and sometimes (it derives from) your prudence.

Many have been routed while crossing a river by an alert enemy of theirs, who waited until they were in the middle of the stream, and then assaulted them on every side; as Caesar did to the Swiss, where he destroyed a fourth part of them, after they had been split by the river. Some time you may find your enemy tired from having pursued you too inconsiderately, so that, finding yourself fresh, and rested, you ought not to lose such an opportunity. In addition to this, if an enemy offers you battle at a good hour of the morning, you can delay going out of your encampment for many hours: and if he has been under arms for a long time, and has lost that first ardor with which he started, you can then fight with him. Scipio and Metellus employed this method in Spain, the first against Hasdrubal, and the other against Sertorius. If the enemy has diminished in strength, either from having divided the Armies, as Scipio (did) in Spain, or from some other cause, you ought to try (your) fortune. The greater part of prudent Captains would rather receive the onrush of the enemy, who impetuously go to assault them, for their fury is easily withstood by firm and resolute men, and that fury which was withstood, easily converts itself into cowardice. Fabius acted thusly against the Samnites and against the Gauls, and was victorious, but his colleague, Decius was killed. Some who feared the virtue of their enemy, have begun the battle at an hour near nightfall, so that if their men were defeated, they might be able to be protected by its darkness and save themselves. Some, having known that the enemy Army, because of certain superstitions, does not want to undertake fighting at such a time, selected that time for battle, and won: which Caesar did in Gaul against Ariovistus, and Vespatianus in Syria against the Jews. The greater and more important awareness that a Captain ought to have, is (to see) that he has about him, men loyal and most expert in war, and prudent, with whom he counsels continually, and discusses his forces and those of the enemy with them: which are the greater in number, which are better armed or better trained, which are more apt to suffer deprivation, which to confide in more, the infantry or the cavalry. Also, they consider the location in which they are, and if it is more suitable for the enemy than for themselves; which of them has the better convenience of supply; whether it is better to delay the engagement or undertake it, and what benefit the weather might give you or take away from them; for often when the soldiers see the war becoming long, they become irritable, and weary from hard work and tedium, will abandon you. Above all, it is important for the Captain to know the enemy, and who he has around him: if he is foolhardy or cautious: if timid or audacious. See whether you can trust the auxiliary soldiers. And above all, you ought to guard against leading an army into battle which is afraid, or distrustful in any way of victory, for the best indication of defeat is when one believes he cannot win. And, therefore, in this case, you ought to avoid an engagement, either by doing as Fabius Maximus did, who, by encamping in strong places, did not give Hannibal courage to go and meet him, or by believing that the enemy, also in strong places, should come to meet you, you should depart from the field, and divide your forces among your towns, so that the tedium of capturing them will tire him.

Zanobi: Can he not avoid the engagement in other ways than by dividing it (the army) into several parts, and putting them in towns?

Fabrizio: I believe at another time I have discussed with some of you that whoever is in the field, cannot avoid an engagement if he has an enemy who wants to fight in any case; and he has but one remedy, and that is to place himself with his Army at least fifty miles distant from his adversary, so as to be in time to get out of his way if he should come to meet him. And Fabius Maximus never avoided an engagement with Hannibal, but wanted it at his advantage; and Hannibal did not presume to be able to overcome him by going to meet him in the places where he was encamped. But if he supposed he could defeat him, it was necessary for Fabius to undertake an engagement with him in any case, or to flee. Phillip, King of Macedonia, he who was the father of Perseus, coming to war with the Romans, placed his encampment on a very high mountain so as not to have an engagement with them; but the Romans went to meet him on that mountain, and routed him. Vercingetorix, a Captain of the Gauls, in order to avoid an engagement with Caesar, who unexpectedly had crossed the river, placed himself miles distant with his forces. The Venetians in our times, if they did not want to come to an engagement with the King of France, ought not to have waited until the French Army had crossed the Adda, but should have placed themselves distant from him, as did Vercingetorix: whence, having waited for him, they did not know how to take the opportunity of undertaking an engagement during the crossing, nor how to avoid it; for the French being near to them, as the Venetians decamped, assaulted and routed them. And so it is, that an engagement cannot be avoided if the enemy at all events wants to undertake it. Nor does anyone cite Fabius, for he avoided an engagement in cases like that, just as much as did Hannibal. It often happens that your soldiers are not willing to fight, and you know that because of their number or the location, or from some other cause, you have a disadvantage, and would like them to change their minds. It also happens that necessity or opportunity constrains you to (come to) an engagement, and that your soldiers are discontent and little disposed to fight, whence it is necessary for you in one case to frighten them, and in the other to excite them. In the first instance, if persuasion is not enough, there is no better way to have both those who fight and those who would not believe you, than to give some of them over to the enemy as plunder. It may also be well to do with cunning that which happened to Fabius Maximus at home. The Army of Fabius desired [as you know] to fight with the Army of Hannibal: his Master of cavalry had the same desire. It did not seem proper to Fabius to attempt the battle, so that in order to dispel such (desires), he had to divide the Army. Fabius kept his men in the encampments: and the other (the Master of cavalry) going forth, and coming into great danger, would have been routed, if Fabius had not succored him. By this example, the Master of the cavalry, together with the entire army, realized it was a wise course to obey Fabius. As to exciting them to fight, it is well to make them angry at the enemy, by pointing out that (the enemy) say slanderous things of them, and showing them to have with their intelligence (in the enemy camp) and having corrupted some part, to encamp on the side where they see the enemy, and undertake some light skirmishes with them; because things that are seen daily are more easily disparaged. By showing yourself indignant, and by making an oration in which you reproach them for their laziness, you make them so ashamed by saying you want to fight only if they do not accompany you. And above everything, to have this awareness, if you want to make the soldiers obstinate in battle, not to permit them to send home any of their possessions, or settle in any place, until the war ends, so that they understand that if flight saves them their lives, it will not save them their possessions, the love of the latter, not less than the former, renders men obstinate in defense.

Zanobi: You have told how soldiers can be made to turn and fight, by talking to them. Do you mean by this that he has to talk to the entire Army, or to its Heads?

Fabrizio: To persuade or dissuade a few from something, is very easy; for if words are not enough, you can use authority and force: but the difficulty is to take away a sinister idea from a multitude, whether it may be in agreement or contrary to your own opinion, where only words can be used, which, if you want to persuade everyone, must be heard by everyone. Captains, therefore, must be excellent Orators, for without knowing how to talk to the entire Army, good things can only be done with difficulty. Which, in these times of ours, is completely done away with. Read the life (biography) of Alexander the Great, and see how many times it was necessary to harangue and speak publicly to the Army; otherwise he could never have led them [having become rich and full of plunder] through the deserts of Arabia and into India with so much hardship and trouble; for infinite numbers of things arose by which an Army is ruined if a Captain does not know how or is not accustomed to talking to it; for this speaking takes away fear, incites courage, increases obstinacy, and sweeps away deceptions, promises rewards, points out dangers and the ways to avoid them, reprimands, begs, threatens, fills with hope, praises, slanders, and does all those things by which human passion is extinguished or enkindled. Whence that Prince or Republic planning to raise a new army, and to give this army reputation, ought to accustom the soldiers to listen to the talk of the Captain, and the Captain to know how to talk to them. Religion was (also) of much value in keeping the ancient soldiers well disposed and an oath was given to (taken by) them when they came into the army; for whenever they made a mistake, they were threatened not only by those evils that can be feared by men, but also by those that can be expected from the Deity. This practice, mixed with other religious means, often made an entire enterprise easy for the ancient Captains, and would always be so whenever religion was feared and observed. Sertorius availed himself of this when he told of talking with a Hind (female stag), which promised him victory on the part of the Deity. Sulla was said to talk with a Statue which he had taken from the Temple of Apollo. Many have told of God appearing to them in their sleep, and admonishing them to fight. In the times of our fathers, Charles the seventh, King of France, in the war he waged against the English, was said to counsel with a young girl sent by God, who is called the Maid of France, and who was the cause for victory. You can also take means to make your (soldiers) value the enemy little, as Agesilaus the Spartan did, who showed his soldiers some Persians in the nude, so that seeing their delicate members, they should have no cause for being afraid of them. Some have constrained them to fight from necessity, by removing from their paths all hope of saving themselves, except through victory. This is the strongest and the best provision that can be made when you want to make your soldiers obstinate. Which obstinacy is increased by the confidence and the love either of the Captain or of the Country. Confidence is instilled by arms organization, fresh victories, and the knowledge of the Captain. Love of Country springs from nature: that of the Captain from (his) virtue more than any other good event. Necessities can be many, but that is the strongest, which constrains you either to win or to die.

FIFTH BOOK

Fabrizio: I have shown you how to organize an army to battle another army which is seen posted against you, and I have told you how it is overcome, and also of the many circumstances which can occur because of the various incidents surrounding it, so that it appears to me now to be the time to show you how to organize an army against an enemy which is unseen, but which you are continually afraid will assault you. This happens when marching through country which is hostile, or suspected (of being so). And first you have to understand that a Roman Army ordinarily always sent ahead some groups of cavalry as observers for the march. Afterwards the right wing followed. After this came all the wagons which pertained to it. After those, another Legion, and next its wagons. After these come the left wing with its wagon in the rear, and the remainder of the cavalry followed in the last part. This was in effect the manner in which one ordinarily marched. And if it happened that the Army should be assaulted on the march in front or from the rear, they quickly caused all the wagons to be withdrawn either on the right, or on the left, according as it happened, or rather as best they could depending on the location, and all the forces together, free from their baggage, set up a front on that side from which the enemy was coming. If they were assaulted on the flank, they would withdraw the wagons to the side which was secure, and set up a front on the other. This method being good, and prudently conducted, appears to me ought to be imitated, sending cavalry ahead to observe the country, then having four battalions, having them march in line, and each with its wagons in the rear.

And as the wagons are of two kinds, that is, those pertaining to individual soldiers, and the public ones for use by the whole camp, I would divide the public wagons into four parts, and assign a part to each Battalion, also dividing the artillery and all the unarmed men, so that each one of those armed should have its equal share of impedimenta. But as it sometimes happens that one marches in a country not only suspect, but hostile in fact, that you are afraid of being attacked hourly, in order to go on more securely, you are compelled to change the formation of the march, and go on in the regular way, so that in some unforeseen place, neither the inhabitants nor the Army can injure you. In such a case, the ancient Captains usually went on with the Army in squares, for such they called these formations, not because it was entirely square, but because it was capable of fighting on four sides, and they said that they were going prepared either for marching or for battle. I do not want to stray far from this method, and want to arrange my two Battalions, which I have taken as a rule for an Army, in this manner.

If you want, therefore, to walk securely through the enemy country, and be able to respond from every side, if you had been assaulted by surprise, and wanting, in accordance with the ancients, to bring it into a square, I would plan to make a square whose hollow was two hundred arm lengths on every side in this manner. I would first place the flanks, each distant from the other by two hundred twelve arm lengths, and would place five companies in each flank in a file along its length, and distant from each other three arm lengths; these would occupy their own space, each company occupying (a space) forty arm lengths by two hundred twelve arm lengths. Between the front and rear of these two flanks, I would place another ten companies, five on each side, arranging them in such a way that four should be next to the front of the right flank, and five at the rear of the left flank, leaving between each one an interval (gap) of four arm lengths: one of which should be next to the front of the left flank, and one at the rear of the right flank. And as the space existing between the one flank and the other is two hundred twelve arm lengths, and these companies placed alongside each other by their width and not length, they would come to occupy, with the intervals, one hundred thirty four arm lengths, (and) there would be between the four companies placed on the front of the right flank, and one placed on the left, a remaining space of seventy eight arm lengths, and a similar space be left among the companies placed in the rear parts; and there would be no other difference, except that one space would be on the rear side toward the right wing, the other would be on the front side toward the left wing. In the space of seventy eight arm lengths in front, I would place all the ordinary Veliti, and in that in the rear the extraordinary Veliti, who would come to be a thousand per space. And if you want that the space taken up by the Army should be two hundred twelve arm lengths on every side, I would see that five companies are placed in front, and those that are placed in the rear, should not occupy any space already occupied by the flanks, and therefore I would see that the five companies in the rear should have their front touch the rear of their flanks, and those in front should have their rear touch the front (of their flanks), so that on every side of that army, space would remain to receive another company. And as there are four spaces, I would take four banners away from the extraordinary pikemen and would put one on every corner: and the two banners of the aforementioned pikemen left to me, I would place in the middle of the hollow of their army (formed) in a square of companies, at the heads of which the general Captain would remain with his men around him. And as these companies so arranged all march in one direction, but not all fight in one, in putting them together, one has to arrange which sides are not guarded by other companies during the battle. And, therefore, it ought to be considered that the five compa- nies in front protect all the other sides, except the front; and therefore these have to be assembled in an orderly manner (and) with the pikemen in front. The five companies behind protect all the sides, except the side in the back; and therefore ought to be assembled so that the pikemen are in the rear, as we will demonstrate in its place. The five companies on the right flank protect all the sides, from the right flank outward. The five on the left, engird all the sides, from the left flank outward: and therefore in arranging the companies, the pikemen ought to be placed so that they turn by that flank which is uncovered. And as the Heads of Ten are placed in the front and rear, so that when they have to fight, all the army and its members are in their proper places, the manner of accomplishing this was told when we discussed the methods of arranging the companies. I would divide the artillery, and one part I would place outside the right flank, and the other at the left. I would send the light cavalry ahead to reconnoiter the country. Of the men-at-arms, I would place part in the rear on the right wing, and part on the left, distant forty arms lengths from the companies. And no matter how you arrange your Army, you have to take up [as the cavalry] this general (rule), that you have to place them always either in the rear or on the flanks. Whoever places them ahead in front of the Army must do one of two things: either he places them so far ahead, that if they are repulsed they have so much room to give them time to be able to obtain shelter for themselves from your infantry and not collide with them; or to arrange them (the infantry) with so many intervals, that by means of them the cavalry can enter among them without disorganizing them. Let not anyone think little of this instruction, because many, not being aware of this, have been ruined, and have been disorganized and routed by themselves. The wagons and the unarmed men are placed in the plaza that exists within the Army, and so compartmented, that they easily make way for whoever wants to go from one side to the other, or from one front of the Army to the other. These companies, without artillery and cavalry, occupy two hundred eighty two arm lengths of space on the outside in every direction. And as this square is composed of two Battalions, it must be devised as to which part one Battalion makes up, and which part the other. And since the Battalions are called by number, and each of them has [as you know] ten companies and a general Head, I would have the first Battalion place its first five companies in the front, the other five on the left flank, and the Head should be in the left angle of the front. The first five companies of the second Battalion then should be placed on the right flank, and the other five in the rear, and the Head should be in the right angle, who would undertake the office of the Tergiduttore.

The Army organized in this manner is ready to move, and in its movement should completely observe this arrangement: and without doubt it is secure from all the tumults of the inhabitants. Nor ought the Captain make other provisions against these tumultuous assaults, than sometime to give a commission to some cavalry or band of Veliti to put them in their place. Nor will it ever happen that these tumultuous people will come to meet you within the drawing of a sword or pike, because disorderly people are afraid of order; and it will always be seen that they make a great assault with shouts and noises without otherwise approaching you in the way of yelping dogs around a mastiff. Hannibal, when he came to harm from the Romans in Italy, passed through all of France, and always took little account of the tumults of the French. When you want to march, you must have levellers and men with pick axes ahead who clear the road for you, and who are well protected by that cavalry sent ahead to reconnoiter. An Army will march in this order ten miles a day, and enough Sun (light will remain for them to dine and camp, since ordinarily an Army marches twenty miles. If it happens that it is assaulted by an organized Army, this assault cannot arise suddenly, because an organized Army travels at its own rate (step), so that you are always in time to reorganize for the engagement, and quickly bring yourself to that formation, or similar to that formation of the Army, which I showed you above. For if you are assaulted on the front side, you do nothing except (to have) the artillery in the flanks and the cavalry behind come forward and take those places and with those distances mentioned above. The thousand Veliti who are forward, come forth from their positions, and dividing into groups of a hundred, enter into their places between the cavalry and the wings of the Army. Then, into the voids left by them, enter the two bands of extraordinary pikemen which I had placed in the plaza of the Army. The thousand Veliti that I had placed in the rear depart from there, and distribute themselves among the flanks of the companies to strengthen them: and from the open space they leave all the wagons and unarmed men issue forth and place themselves at the rear of the companies. The plaza, therefore, remains vacant as everyone has gone to their places, and the five companies that I placed in the rear of the Army come forward through the open void that exists between the one and the other flank, and march toward the company in the front, and the three approach them at forty arm lengths with equal intervals between one another, and two remain behind distant another forty arm lengths. This formation can be organized quickly, and comes to be almost the same as the first disposition of the Army which we described before: and if it becomes more straitened in the front, it becomes larger in the flanks, which does not weaken it. But as the five companies in the back have their pikemen in the rear for the reasons mentioned above, it is necessary to have them come from the forward part, if you want them to get behind the front of the Army; and, therefore, one must either make them turn company by company, as a solid body, or make them enter quickly between the ranks of the shieldbearers (swordsmen), and bring them forward; which method is more swift and less disorderly than to make them turn. And thus you ought to do with all those who are in the rear in every kind of assault, as I will show you. If it should happen that the enemy comes from the rear, the first thing that ought to be done is to have everyone turn to face the enemy, so that at once the front of the army becomes the rear, and the rear the front. Then all those methods of organizing the front should be followed, which I mentioned above. If the enemy attacks on the right flank, the entire army ought to be made to face in that direction, and then those things ought to be done to strengthen that (new) front which were mentioned above, so that the cavalry, the Veliti, and the artillery are in the position assigned in this front. There is only this difference, that in the changing of fronts, of those who move about, some have to go further, and some less. It is indeed true that when a front is made of the right flank, the Veliti would have to enter the intervals (gaps) that exist between the wings of the Army, and the cavalry would be those nearer to the left flank, in the position of those who would have to enter into the two bands of extraordinary pikemen placed in the center. But before they enter, the wagons and unarmed men stationed at the openings, should clear the plaza and retire behind the left flank, which then becomes the rear of the army. And the other

Veliti who should be placed in the rear according to the original arrangement, in this case should not be changed, as that place should not remain open, which, from being the rear, would become a flank. All the other things ought to be done as was said concerning the first front.

What has been said concerning making a front from the right flank, is intended also in making one from the left flank, since the same arrangements ought to be observed. If the enemy should happen to be large and organized to assault you on two sides, the two sides on which he assaults you ought to be strengthened from the two that are not assaulted, doubling the ranks in each one, and distributing the artillery, Veliti, and cavalry among each side. If he comes from three or four sides, it must be either you or he lacks prudence, for if you were wise, you would never put yourself on the side where the enemy could assault you from three or four sides with large and organized forces, and if he wanted to attack you in safety he must be so large and assault you on each side with a force almost as large as you have in your entire Army. And if you are so little prudent that you put yourself in the midst of the territory and forces of an enemy, who has three times the organized forces that you have, you cannot complain if evil happens to you, except of yourself. If it happens, not by your fault, but by some misadventure, the injury will be without shame, and it will happen to you as it did to the Scipios in Spain, and the Hasdrubal in Italy. But if the enemy has a much larger force than you, and in order to disorganize you wants to assault you on several sides, it will be his foolishness and his gamble; for to do this, he must go (spread) himself thin, that you can always attack on one side and resist on another, and in a brief time ruin him. This method of organizing an Army which is not seen, but who is feared, is necessary, and it is a most useful thing to accustom your soldiers to assemble, and march in such order, and in marching arrange themselves to fight according to the first front (planned), and then return to marching formation, from that make a front from the rear, and then from the flank, and from that return to the original formation. These exercises and accustomization are necessary matters if you want a disciplined and trained Army.

Captains and Princes have to work hard at these things: nor is military discipline anything else, than to know how to command and how to execute these things, nor is a disciplined Army anything else, than an army which is well trained in these arrangements; nor would it be possible for anyone in these times who should well employ such discipline ever to be routed. And if this square formation which I have described is somewhat difficult, such difficulty is necessary, if you take it up as exercise; since knowing how to organize and maintain oneself well in this, one would afterwards know how to manage more easily those which not be as difficult.

Zanobi: I believe as you say, that these arrangements are very necessary, and by myself, I would not know what to add or leave out. It is true that I desire to know two things from you: the one, when you want to make a front from the rear or from a flank, and you want them to turn, whether the command is given by voice or by sound (bugle call): the other, whether those you sent ahead to clear the roads in order to make a path for the Army, ought to be soldiers of your companies, or other lowly people assigned to such practices.

Fabrizio: Your first question is very important, for often the commands of the Captain are not very well understood or poorly interpreted, have disorganized their Army; hence the voices with which they command in (times of) danger, ought to be loud and clear. And if you command with sounds (bugle calls), it ought to be done so that they are so different from each other that one cannot be mistaken for another; and if you command by voice, you ought to be alert to avoid general words, and use particular ones, and of the particular ones avoid those which might be able to be interpreted in an incorrect manner. Many times saying "go back, go back," has caused an Army to be ruined: therefore this expression ought to be avoided, and in its place use "Retreat." If you want them to turn so as to change the front, either from the rear or from the flank, never use "Turn around," but say, "To the left," "To the right," "To the rear," "To the front." So too, all the other words have to be simple and clear, as "Hurry," "Hold still," "Forward," "Return." And all those things which can be done by words are done, the others

are done by sounds (calls). As to the (road) clearers, which is
your second question, I would have this job done by my own soldiers, as much because the ancient military did so, as also
because there would be fewer unarmed men and less impediments in the army: and I would draw the number needed from
every company, and I would have them take up the tools suitable for clearing, and leave their arms in those ranks that are
closest to them, which would carry them so that if the enemy
should come, they would have nothing to do but take them up
again and return to their ranks.

Zanobi: Who would carry the clearing equipment?

Fabrizio: The wagons assigned to carry such equipment.

Zanobi: I'm afraid you have never led these soldiers of ours
to dig.

Fabrizio: Everything will be discussed in its place. For now
I want to leave these parts alone, and discuss the manner of living of the Army, for it appears to me that having worked them
so hard, it is time to refresh and restore it with food. You have
to understand that a Prince ought to organize his army as expe-
ditiously as possible, and take away from it all those things that
add burdens to it and make the enterprise difficult. Among
those that cause more difficulty, are to have to keep the army
provided with wine and baked bread. The ancients did not think
of wine, for lacking it, they drank water tinted with a little vinegar, and not wine. They did not cook bread in ovens, as is customary throughout the cities; but they provided flour, and every
soldier satisfied himself of that in his own way, having lard and
grease for condiment, which gave flavor to the bread they made,
and which kept them strong. So that the provisions of living
(eating) for the army were Flour, Vinegar, Lard (Bacon) and
Grease (Lard), and Barley for the horses. Ordinarily, they had
herds of large and small beasts that followed the Army, which
[as they did not need to be carried] did not impede them much.
This arrangement permitted an ancient Army to march, sometimes for many days, through solitary and difficult places without suffering hardship of (lack of) provisions, for it lived from
things which could be drawn behind. The contrary happens in
modern Armies, which, as they do not want to lack wine and eat

baked bread in the manner that those at home do, and of which they cannot make provision for long, often are hungry; or even if they are provided, it is done with hardship and at very great expense. I would therefore return my Army to this form of living, and I would not have them eat other bread than that which they should cook for themselves. As to wine, I would not prohibit its drinking, or that it should come into the army, but I would not use either industry or any hard work to obtain it, and as to other provisions, I would govern myself entirely as the ancients. If you would consider this matter well, you will see how much difficulty is removed, and how many troubles and hardships an army and a Captain avoid, and what great advantage it will give any enterprise which you may want to undertake.

Zanobi: We have overcome the enemy in the field, and then marched on his country: reason wants that there be no booty, ransoming of towns, prisoners taken. Yet I would like to know how the ancients governed themselves in these matters.

Fabrizio: Here, I will satisfy you. I believe you have considered [since I have at another time discussed this with some of you] that modern wars impoverish as much those Lords who win, as those who lose; for if one loses the State, the other loses his money and (movable) possessions. Which anciently did not happen, as the winner of a war (then) was enriched. This arises from not keeping track in these times of the booty (acquired), as was done anciently, but everything is left to the direction of the soldiers. This method makes for two very great disorders: the one, that of which I have spoken: the other, that a soldier becomes more desirous of booty and less an observer of orders: and it has often been said that the cupidity for booty has made him lose who had been victorious. The Romans, however, who were Princes in this matter, provided for both these inconveniences, ordering that all the booty belong to the public, and that hence the public should dispense it as it pleased. And so they had Quaestors in the Army, who were, as we would say, chamberlains, to whom all the ransoms and booty was given to hold: from which the Consul served himself to give the soldiers their regular pay, to help the wounded and infirm, and to provide for the other needs of the army. The Consul could indeed, and often did, concede a booty to the soldiers, but this concession did not cause disorders; for when the (enemy) army was routed, all the booty was placed in the middle and was distributed to each person, according to the merits of each. This method made for the soldiers attending to winning and not robbing, and the Roman legions defeating the enemy but not pursuing him: for they never departed from their orders: only the cavalry and lightly armed men pursued him, unless there were other soldiers than legionnaires, which, if the booty would have been kept by whoever acquired it, it was neither possible nor reasonable to (expect to) hold the Legion firm, and would bring on many dangers. From this it resulted, therefore, that the public was enriched, and every Consul brought, with his triumphs, much treasure into the Treasury, which (consisted) entirely of ransoms and booty. Another thing well considered by the ancients, was the pay they gave to each soldier: they wanted a third part to be placed next to him who carried the flag of the company, who never was given any except that furnished by the war. They did this for two reasons: The first so that the soldier would make capital (save) of his pay: for the greater part of them being young and irresponsible, the more they had, the more they spent without need to. The other part because, knowing that their movable possessions were next to the flag, they would be forced to have greater care, and defend it with greater obstinacy: and thus this method made them savers, and strong. All of these things are necessary to observe if you want to bring the military up to your standards.

Zanobi: I believe it is not possible for an army while marching from place to place not to encounter dangerous incidents, (and) where the industry of the Captain and the virtue of the soldier is needed if they are to be avoided; therefore, if you should have something that occurs to you, I would take care to listen.

Fabrizio: I will willingly content you, especially as it is necessary, if I want to give you complete knowledge of the practice. The Captains, while they march with the Army, ought, above everything else, to guard against ambushes, which may happen in two ways: either you enter into them while marching, or the enemy cunningly draws you into them without your being aware of it. In the first case, if you want to avoid them, it is necessary to send ahead double the guard, who reconnoiter the country. And the more the country is suitable for ambush, as are wooded and mountainous countries, the more diligence ought to be used, for the enemy always place themselves either in woods or behind a hill. And, just as by not foreseeing an ambush you will be ruined, so by foreseeing it you will not be harmed. Birds or dust have often discovered the enemy, for where the enemy comes to meet you, he will always raise a great dust which will point out his coming to you. Thus often a Captain when he sees in a place whence he ought to pass, pigeons taking off and other birds flying about freely, circling and not setting, has recognized this to be the place of an enemy ambush, and knowing this has sent his forces forward, saving himself and injuring the enemy. As to the second case, being drawn into it [which our men call being drawn into a trap] you ought to look out not to believe readily those things that appear to be less reasonable than they should be: as would be (the case) if an enemy places some booty before you, you would believe that to be (an act of) love, but would conceal deceit inside it. If many enemies are driven out by few of your man: if only a few of the enemy assault you: if the enemy takes to sudden and unreasonable flight: in such cases, you ought always to be afraid of deceit; and you should never believe that the enemy does not know his business, rather, if you want to deceive yourself less and bring on less danger, the more he appears weak, the more enemy appears more cautious, so much the more ought you to esteem (be wary) of him. And in this you have to use two different means, since you have to fear him with your thoughts and arrangements, but by words and other external demonstrations show him how much you disparage him; for this latter method causes your soldiers to have more hope in obtaining the victory, the former makes you more cautious and less apt to be deceived. And you have to understand that when you march through enemy country, you face more and greater dangers than in undertaking an engagement. And therefore, when marching, a Captain ought to double his diligence, and the first thing he ought to do, is to have all the country through which he marches described and depicted, so that he will know the places, the numbers, the distances, the roads, the mountains, the rivers, the marshes, and all their characteristics. And in getting to know this, in diverse ways one must have around him different people who know the places, and question them with diligence, and contrast their information, and make notes according as it checks out. He ought to send cavalry ahead, and with them prudent Heads, not so much to discover the enemy as to reconnoiter the country, to see whether it checks with the places and with the information received from them. He ought also to send out guides, guarded (kept loyal) by hopes of reward and fear of punishment. And above all, he ought to see to it that the Army does not know to which sides he guides them, since there is nothing more useful in war, than to keep silent (about) the things that have to be done. And so that a sudden assault does not disturb your soldiers, you ought to advise them to be prepared with their arms, since things that are foreseen cause less harm. Many have [in order to avoid the confusion of the march] placed the wagons and the unarmed men under the banners, and commanded them to follow them, so that having to stop or retire during the march, they are able to do so more easily: which I approve very much as something useful. He ought also to have an awareness during the march, that one part of the Army does not detach itself from another, or that one (part) going faster and the other more slowly, the Army does not become compacted (jumbled), which things cause disorganization. It is necessary, therefore, to place the Heads along the sides, who should maintain the steps uniform, restraining those which are too fast, and hastening the slow; which step cannot be better regulated than by sound (music). The roads ought to be widened, so that at least one company can always move in order. The customs and characteristics of the enemy ought to be considered, and if he wants to assault you in the morning, noon, or night, and if he is more powerful in infantry or cavalry, from what you have learned, you may organize and prepare yourself. But let us come to some incident in particular. It sometimes happens that as you are taking yourself away from in front of the enemy because you judge yourself to be inferior (to him), and therefore do not want to come to an engagement with him, he comes upon your rear as you arrive at the banks of a river, which causes you to lose times in its crossing, so that the enemy is about to join up and combat with you. There have been some who have found themselves in such a peril, their army girded on the rear side by a ditch, and filling it with tow, have set it afire, then have passed on with the army without being able to be impeded by the enemy, he being stopped by that fire which was in between.

Zanobi: And it is hard for me to believe that this fire can check him, especially as I remember to have heard that Hanno, the Carthaginian, when he was besieged by the enemy, girded himself on that side from which he wanted to make an eruption with wood, and set fire to it. Whence the enemy not being intent to guard that side, had his army pass over the flames, having each (soldier) protect his face from the fire and smoke with his shield.

Fabrizio: You say well; but consider what I have said and what Hanno did: for I said that he dug a ditch and filled it with tow, so that whoever wanted to pass had to contend with the ditch and the fire. Hanno made the fire without a ditch, and as he wanted to pass through it did not make it very large (strong), since it would have impeded him even without the ditch. Do you not know that Nabidus, the Spartan, when he was besieged in Sparta by the Romans, set fire to part of his own town in order to stop the passage of the Romans, who had already entered inside? and by those flames not only stopped their passage, but pushed them out. But let us return to our subject. Quintus Luttatius, the Roman, having the Cimbri at his rear, and arriving at a river, so that the enemy should give him time to cross, made as if to give him time to combat him, and therefore feigned to make camp there, and had ditches dug, and some pavilions raised, and sent some horses to the camps to be shod: so that the Cimbri believing he was encamping, they also encamped, and divided themselves into several parts to provide themselves with food: of which Luttatius becoming aware, he crossed the river without being able to be impeded by them.

Some, in order to cross a river, not having a bridge, have diverted it, and having drawn a part of it in their rear, the other then
became so low that they crossed it easily. If the rivers are rapid,
(and) desiring that the infantry should cross more safely, the
more capable horses are placed on the side above which holds
back the water, and another part below which succor the
infantry if any, in crossing, should be overcome by the river.
Rivers that are not forded, are crossed by bridges, boats, and
rafts: and it is therefore well to have skills in your Armies capable of doing all these things. It sometimes happens that in crossing a river, the enemy on the opposite bank impedes you. If you
want to overcome this difficulty there is no better example
known than that of Caesar, who, having his army on the bank of
a river in Gaul, and his crossing being impeded by Vercingetorix, the Gaul, who had his forces on the other side of the river,
marched for several days along the river, and the enemy did the
same. And Caesar having made an encampment in a woody
place (and) suitable to conceal his forces, withdrew three
cohorts from every Legion, and had them stop in that place,
commanding then that as soon as he should depart, they should
throw a bridge across and fortify it, and he with the rest of his
forces continued the march: Whence Vercingetorix seeing the
number of Legions, and believing that no part had remained
behind, also continued the march: but Caesar, as soon as he
thought the bridge had been completed, turned back, and finding everything in order, crossed the river without difficulty.

Zanobi: Do you have any rule for recognizing the fords?

Fabrizio: Yes, we have. The river, in that part between the
stagnant water and the current, always looks like a line to whoever looks at it, is shallower, and is a place more suitable for
fording than elsewhere, for the river always places more material, and in a pack, which it draws (with it) from the bottom.
Which thing, as it has been experienced many times, is very
true.

Zanobi: If it happens that the river has washed away the bottom of the ford, so that horses sink, what remedy do you have?

Fabrizio: Make grids of wood, and place them on the bottom
of the river, and cross over those. But let us pursue our discus-

sion. If it happens that a Captain with his army is led (caught) between two mountains, and has but two ways of saving himself, either that in front, or the one in the rear, and both being occupied by the enemy, has, as a remedy, to do what some have done in the past, which is to dig a large ditch, difficult to cross, and show the enemy that by it you want to be able to hold him with all his forces, without having to fear those forces in the rear for which the road in front remains open. The enemy believing this, fortifies himself on the side open, and abandons the (side) closed, and he then throws a wooden bridge, planned for such a result, over the ditch, and without any impediment, passes on that side and freed himself from the hands of the enemy. Lucius Minutius, the Roman Consul, was in Liguria with the Armies, and had been enclosed between certain mountains by the enemy, from which he could not go out. He therefore sent some soldiers of Numidia, whom he had in his army, who were badly armed, and mounted on small and scrawny horses, toward those places which were guarded by the enemy, and the first sight of whom caused the enemy to assemble to defend the pass: but then when they saw those forces poorly organized, and also poorly mounted, they esteemed them little and loosened their guard. As soon as the Numidians saw this, giving spurs to their horses and attacking them, they passed by without the enemy being able to take any remedy; and having passed, they wasted and plundered the country, constraining the enemy to leave the pass free to the army of Lucius. Some Captain, who has found himself assaulted by a great multitude of the enemy, has tightened his ranks, and given the enemy the faculty of completely surrounding him, and then has applied force to that part which he has recognized as being weaker, and has made a path in that way, and saved himself. Marcantonio, while retiring before the army of the Parthians, became aware that every day at daybreak as he moved, the enemy assaulted him, and infested him throughout the march: so that he took the course of not departing before midday. So that the Parthians, believing he should not want to decamp that day returned to their quarters, and Marcantonio was able then for the remainder of the day to march without being molested. This same man, to escape the darts of the Parthians, commanded that, when the Parthians came toward them, they should kneel, and the second rank of the company should place their shields on the heads of (those in the) first, the third on (those of the) second, the fourth on the third, and so on successively: so that the entire Army came to be as under a roof, and protected from the darts of the enemy. This is as much as occurs to me to tell you of what can happen to an army when marching: therefore, if nothing else occurs to you, I will pass on to another part.

SIXTH BOOK

Zanobi: I believe it is well, since the discussion ought to be changed, that Battista take up his office, and I resign mine; and in this case we would come to imitate the good Captains, according as I have already learned here from the Lord, who place the best soldiers in the front and in the rear of the Army, as it appears necessary to them to have those in the front who bravely enkindle the battle, and those in the rear who bravely sustain it. Cosimo, therefore, begun this discussion prudently, and Battista will prudently finish it. Luigi and I have come in between these. And as each one of us has taken up his part willingly, so too I believe Battista is about to close it.

Battista: I have allowed myself to be governed up to now, so too I will allow myself (to be governed) in the future. Be content, therefore, (my) Lords, to continue your discussions, and if we interrupt you with these questions (practices), you have to excuse us.

Fabrizio: You do me, as I have already told you, a very great favor, since these interruptions of yours do not take away my imagination, rather they refresh it. But if we want to pursue our subject I say, that it is now time that we quarter this Army of ours, since you know that everything desires repose, and safety; since to repose oneself, and not to repose safely, is not complete (perfect) repose. I am afraid, indeed, that you should not desire that I should first quarter them, then had them march, and lastly to fight, and we have done the contrary. Necessity has led us to this, for in wanting to show when marching, how an army turns from a marching formation to that of battle, it was necessary first to show how they were organized for battle. But returning to our subject I say, that if you want the encampment to be safe, it must be Strong and Organized. The industry of the Captain makes it Organized: Arts or the site make it Strong. The Greeks sought strong locations, and never took positions where there was neither grottoes (caves), or banks of rivers, or a multitude of trees, or other natural cover which should protect them. But the Romans did not encamp safely so much from the location as by arts, nor ever made an encampment in places where they should not have been able to spread out all their forces, according to their discipline. From this resulted that the Romans were always able to have one form of encampment, for they wanted the site to obey them, and not they the site. The Greeks were not able to observe this, for as they obeyed the site, and the sites changing the formation, it behooved them that they too should change the mode of encamping and the form of their encampment. The Romans, therefore, where the site lacked strength, supplied it with (their) art and industry. And since in this narration of mine, I have wanted that the Romans be imitated, I will not depart from their mode of encamping, not, however, observing all their arrangements: but taking (only) that part which at the present time seems appropriate to me. I have often told you that the Romans had two Legions of Roman men in their consular armies, which comprised some eleven thousand infantry of forces sent by friends (allies) to aid them; but they never had more foreign soldiers in their armies than Romans, except for cavalry, which they did not care if they exceeded the number in their Legions; and that in every action of theirs, they place the Legions in the center, and the Auxiliaries on the sides. Which method they observed even when they encamped, as you yourselves have been able to read in those who write of their affairs; and therefore I am not about to narrate in detail how they encamped, but will tell you only how I would at present arrange to encamp my army, and then you will know what part of the Roman methods I have treated. You know that at the encounter of two Roman Legions I have taken two Battalions of six thousand infantry and three hundred cavalry effective for each Battalion, and I have divided them by

companies, by arms, and names. You know that in organizing
the army for marching and fighting, I have not made mention
of other forces, but have only shown that in doubling the
forces, nothing else had to be done but to double the orders
(arrangements).

Since at present I want to show you the manner of encamping, it appears proper to me not to stay only with two Battalions,
but to assemble a fair army, and composed like the Roman of
two Battalions and as many auxiliary forces. I know that the
form of an encampment is more perfect, when a complete army
is quartered: which matter did not appear necessary to me in the
previous demonstration. If I want, therefore, to quarter a fair
(sized) army of twenty four thousand infantry and two thousand
cavalry effectives, being divided into four companies, two of
your own forces and two of foreigners, I would employ this
method. When I had found the site where I should want to
encamp, I would raise the Captain's flag, and around it I would
draw a square which would have each face distant from it fifty
arm lengths, of which each should look out on one of the four
regions of the sky, that is, east, west, south and north, in which
space I would put the quarters of the Captain. And as I believe
it prudent, and because thus the Romans did in good part, I
would divide the armed men from the unarmed, and separate
the men who carry burdens from the unburdened ones. I would
quarter all or a greater part of the armed men on the east side,
and the unarmed and burdened ones on the west side, making
the east the front and the west the rear of the encampment, and
the south and north would be the flanks. And to distinguish the
quarters of the armed men, I would employ this method. I
would run a line from the Captain's flag, and would lead it east-
erly for a distance of six hundred eighty (680) arm lengths. I
would also run two other lines which I would place in the middle of it, and be of the same length as the former, but distant
from each of them by fifteen arm lengths, at the extremity of
which, I would want the east gate to be (placed): and the space
which exists between the two extreme (end) lines, I would make
a road that would go from the gate to the quarters of the
Captain, which would be thirty arm lengths in width and six

hundred thirty (630) long [since the Captain's quarters would occupy fifty arm lengths] and call this the Captain's Way. I would then make another road from the south gate up to the north gate, and cross by the head of the Captain's Way, and along the east side of the Captain's quarters which would be one thousand two hundred fifty (1,250) arm lengths long [since it would occupy the entire width of the encampment] and also be thirty arm lengths wide and be called the Cross Way. The quarters of the Captain and these two roads having been designed, therefore the quarters of the two battalions of your own men should begin to be designed; and I would quarter one on the right hand (side) of the Captain's Way, and one on the left. And hence beyond the space which is occupied by the width of the Cross Way, I would place thirty two quarters on the left side of the Captain's Way, and thirty two on the right side, leaving a space of thirty arm lengths between the sixteenth and seventeenth quarters which should serve as a transverse road which should cross through all of the quarters of the battalions, as will be seen in their partitioning. Of these two arrangements of quarters, in the first tents that would be adjacent to the Cross Way, I would quarter the heads of men-at-arms, and since each company has one hundred and fifty men-at-arms, there would be assigned ten men-at-arms to each of the quarters. The area (space) of the quarters of the Heads should be forty arm lengths wide and ten arm lengths long. And it is to be noted that whenever I say width, I mean from south to north, and when I say length, that from west to east. Those of the men-at-arms should be fifteen arm lengths long and thirty wide. In the next fifteen quarters which in all cases are next [which should have their beginning across the transverse road, and which would have the same space as those of the men-at-arms] I would quarter the light cavalry, which, since they are one hundred fifty, ten cavalrymen would be assigned to each quarter, and in the sixteenth which would be left, I would quarter their Head, giving him the same space which is given to the Head of men-at-arms. And thus the quarters of the cavalry of the two battalions would come to place the Captain's Way in the center and give a rule for the quarters of the infantry, as I will narrate. You have noted that I have quartered the three hundred cavalry of each battalion with their heads in thirty two quarters situated on the Captain's Way, and beginning with the Cross Way, and that from the sixteenth to the seventeenth there is a space of thirty arm lengths to make a transverse road. If I want, therefore, to quarter the twenty companies which constitute the two regular Battalions, I would place the quarters of every two companies behind the quarters of the cavalry, each of which should be fifteen arm lengths long and thirty wide, as those of the cavalry, and should be joined on the rear where they touch one another. And in every first quarter of each band that fronts on the Cross Way, I would quarter the Constable of one company, which would come to correspond with the quartering of the Head of the men-at-arms: and their quarters alone would have a space of twenty arm lengths in width and ten in length. And in the other fifteen quarters in each group which follow after this up the Transverse Way, I would quarter a company of infantry on each side, which, as they are four hundred fifty, thirty would be assigned to each quarter. I would place the other fifteen quarters contiguous in each group to those of the cavalry with the same space, in which I would quarter a company of infantry from each group. In the last quarter of each group I would place the Constable of the company, who would come to be adjacent to the Head of the light cavalry, with a space of ten arm lengths long and twenty wide. And thus these first two rows of quarters would be half of cavalry and half of infantry.

And as I want [as I told you in its place] these cavalry to be all effective, and hence without retainers who help taking care of the horses or other necessary things, I would want these infantry quartered behind the cavalry should be obligated to help the owners (of the horses) in providing and taking care of them, and because of this should be exempt from other activities of the camp, which was the manner observed by the Romans. I would also leave behind these quarters on all sides a space of thirty arm lengths to make a road, and I would call one of the First Road on the right hand (side) and the other the First Road on the left, and in each area I would place another row of thirty two double quarters which should face one another on the rear, with the

same spaces as those which I have mentioned, and also divided
at the sixteenth in the same manner to create a Transverse Road,
in which I would quarter in each area four companies of infantry
with the Constables in the front at the head and foot (of each
row). I would also leave on each side another space of thirty arm
lengths to create a road which should be called the Second Road
on the right hand (side) and on the other side the Second Road
on the left; I would place another row in each area of thirty two
double quarters, with the same distances and divisions, in which
I would quarter on every side four companies (of infantry) with
their Constables. And thus there would come to be quartered in
three rows of quarters per area the cavalry and the companies
(of infantry) of the two regular battalions, in the center of which
I would place the Captain's Way. The two battalions of auxiliaries
[since I had them composed of the same men] I would quarter
on each side of these two regular battalions with the same
arrangement of double quarters, placing first a row of quarters
in which I should quarter half with cavalry and half infantry, distant thirty arm lengths from each other, to create two roads
which I should call, one the Third Road on the right hand (side),
the other the Third Road on the left hand. And then I would
place on each side two other rows of quarters, separate but
arranged in the same way, which are those of the regular battalions, which would create two other roads, and all of these would
be called by the number and the band (side) where they should
be situated. So that all this part of the Army would come to be
quartered in twelve rows of double quarters, and on thirteen
roads, counting the Captain's Way and the Cross Way.

I would want a space of one hundred arm lengths all around
left between the quarters and the ditch (moat). And if you count
all those spaces, you will see, that from the middle of the quarters of the Captain to the east gate, there are seven hundred arm
lengths. There remains to us now two spaces, of which one is
from the quarters of the Captain to the south gate, the other
from there to the north gate, each of which comes to be, measuring from the center point, six hundred thirty five (635) arm
lengths. I then subtract from each of these spaces fifty arm
lengths which the quarters of the Captain occupies, and forty

five arm lengths of plaza which I want to give to each side, and thirty arm lengths of road, which divides each of the mentioned spaces in the middle, and a hundred arm lengths which are left on each side between the quarters and the ditch, and there remains in each area a space left for quarters four hundred arm lengths wide and a hundred long, measuring the length to include the space occupied by the Captain's quarters. Dividing the said length in the middle, therefore, there would be on each side of the Captain forty quarters fifty arm lengths long and twenty wide, which would total eighty quarters, in which would be quartered the general Heads of the battalions, the Chamberlains, the Masters of the camps, and all those who should have an office (duty) in the army, leaving some vacant for some foreigners who might arrive, and for those who should fight through the courtesy of the Captain. On the rear side of the Captain's quarters, I would create a road thirty arm lengths wide from north to south, and call it the Front Road, which would come to be located along the eighty quarters mentioned, since this road and the Cross Way would have between them the Captain's quarters and the eighty quarters on their flanks. From this Front Road and opposite to the Captain's quarters, I would create another road which should go from there to the west gate, also thirty arm lengths wide, and corresponding in location and length to the Captain's Way, and I should call it the Way of the Plaza. These two roads being located, I would arrange the plaza where the market should be made, which I would place at the head of the Way of the Plaza, opposite to the Captain's quarters, and next to the Front Road, and would want it to be square, and would allow it a hundred twenty one arm lengths per side. And from the right hand and left hand of the said plaza, I would make two rows of quarters, and each row have eight double quarters, which would take up twelve arm lengths in length and thirty in width so that they should be on each side of the plaza, in which there would be sixteen quarters, and total thirty two all together, in which I would quarter that cavalry left over from the auxiliary battalions, and if this should not be enough, I would assign them some of the quarters about the Captain, and especially those which face the ditch.

It remains for us now to quarter the extraordinary pikemen and Veliti, which every battalion has; which you know, according to our arrangement, in addition to the ten companies (of infantry), each has a thousand extraordinary pikemen, and five hundred Veliti; so that each of the two regular battalions have two thousand extraordinary pikemen, and a thousand extraordinary pikemen, and five hundred Veliti; so that each of the two regular battalions have two thousand extraordinary pikemen, and a thousand extraordinary Veliti, and the auxiliary as many as they; so that one also comes to have to quarter six thousand infantry, all of whom I would quarter on the west side along the ditches. From the point, therefore, of the Front Road, and northward, leaving the space of a hundred arm lengths from those (quarters) to the ditch, I would place a row of five double quarters which would be seventy five arm lengths long and sixty in width: so that with the width divided, each quarters would be allowed fifteen arm lengths for length and thirty for width. And as there would be ten quarters, I would quarter three hundred infantry, assigning thirty infantry to each quarters. Leaving then a space of thirty one arm lengths, I would place another row of five double quarters in a similar manner and with similar spaces, and then another, so that there would be five rows of five double quarters, which would come to be fifty quarters placed in a straight line on the north side, each distant one hundred arm lengths from the ditches, which would quarter one thousand five hundred infantry. Turning then on the left hand side toward the west gate, I would want in all that tract between them and the said gate, five other rows of double quarters, in a similar manner and with the same spaces, [it is true that from one row to the other there would not be more than fifteen arm lengths of space] in which there would also be quartered a thousand five hundred infantry: and thus from the north gate to that on the west, following the ditches, in a hundred quarters, divided into ten rows of five double quarters per row, the extraordinary pikemen and Veliti of the regular battalions would be quartered. And so, too, from the west gate to that on the south, following the ditches, in exactly the same manner, in another ten rows of ten quarters per row, the extraordinary pikemen and Veliti of the auxiliary battalions would be quartered. Their Heads, or rather their Constables, could take those quarters on the side toward the ditches which appeared most convenient for themselves.

I would dispose the artillery all along the embankments of the ditches: and in all the other space remaining toward the west, I would quarter all the unarmed men and all the baggage (impedimenta) of the Camp. And it has to be understood that under this name of impedimenta [as you know] the ancients intended all those carriages (wagons) and all those things which are necessary to an Army, except the soldiers; as are carpenters (wood workers), smiths, blacksmiths, shoe makers, engineers, and bombardiers, and others which should be placed among the number of the armed: herdsmen with their herds of castrated sheep and oxen, which are used for feeding the Army: and in addition, masters of every art (trade), together with public wagons for the public provisions of food and arms. And I would not particularly distinguish their quarters: I would only designate the roads that should not be occupied by them. Then the other spaces remaining between the roads, which would be four, I would assign in general to all the impedimenta mentioned, that is, one to the herdsmen, another to artificers and workmen, another to the public wagons for provisions, and the fourth to the armorers. The roads which I would want left unoccupied would be the Way of the Plaza, the Front Road, and in addition, a road that should be called the Center Road, which should take off at the north and proceed toward the south, and pass through the center of the Way of the Plaza, which, on the west side, should have the same effect as has the Transverse Road on the east side. And in addition to this a Road that should go around the rear along the quarters of the extraordinary pikemen and Veliti. And all these roads should be thirty arm lengths wide. And I would dispose the artillery along the ditches on the rear of the camp.

Battista: I confess I do not understand, and I also do not believe that to say so makes me ashamed, as this is not my profession. nonetheless, I like this organization very much: I would want only that you should resolve these doubts for me. The one, why you make the roads and the spaces around the quarters so wide. The other, which annoys me more, is this, how are these spaces that you designate for quarters to be used.

Fabrizio: You know that I made all the roads thirty arm lengths wide, so that a company of infantry is able to go through them in order (formation): which, if you remember well, I told you that each of these (formations) were twenty five to thirty arm lengths wide. The space between the ditch and the quarters, which is a hundred arm lengths wide, is necessary, since the companies and the artillery can be handled here, through which booty is taken, (and) when space is needed into which to retire, new ditches and embankments are made. The quarters very distant from the ditches are better, for they are more distant from the fires and other things that might be able to draw the enemy to attack them. As to the second question, my intention is not that every space designated by me is covered by only one pavilion, but is to be used as an all-round convenience for those who are quartered, with several or few tents, so long as they do not go outside its limits. And in designing these quarters, the men must be most experienced and excellent architects, who, as soon as the Captain has selected the site, know how to give it form, and divide it, and distinguishing the roads, dividing the quarters with cords and hatchets in such a practical manner, that they might be divided and arranged quickly. And if confusion is not to arise, the camp must always face the same way, so that everyone will know on which Road and in which space he has to find his quarters. And this ought to be observed at all times, in every place, and in a manner that it appears to be a movable City, which, wherever it goes, brings with it the same roads, the same houses, and the same appearance: which cannot be observed by those men who, seeking strong locations, have to change the form according to the variations in the sites. But the Romans made the places strong with ditches, ramparts, and embankments, for they placed a space around the camp, and in front of it they dug a ditch and ordinarily six arm lengths wide and three deep, which spaces they increased according to the (length of) time they resided in the one place, and according as they feared the enemy. For myself, I would not at present erect a stockade (rampart), unless I should want to winter in a place. I would, however, dig the ditch and embankment, not less than that mentioned, but greater according to the necessity. With respect to the artillery, on every side of the encampment, I would have a half circle ditch, from which the artillery should be able to batter on the flanks whoever should come to attack the moats (ditches). The soldiers ought also to be trained in this practice of knowing how to arrange an encampment, and work with them so they may aid him in designing it, and the soldiers quick in knowing their places. And none of these is difficult, as will be told in its proper place. For now I want to pass on to the protection of the camp, which, without the distribution (assignment) of guards, all the other efforts would be useless.

Battista: Before you pass on to the guards, I would want you to tell me, what methods are employed when others want to place the camp near the enemy, for I do not know whether there is time to be able to organize it without danger.

Fabrizio: You have to know this, that no Captain encamps near the enemy, unless he is disposed to come to an engagement whenever the enemy wants; and if the others are so disposed, there is no danger except the ordinary, since two parts of the army are organized to make an engagement, while the other part makes the encampment. In cases like this, the Romans assigned this method of fortifying the quarters to the Triari, while the Principi and the Astati remained under arms. They did this, because the Triari, being the last to combat, were in time to leave the work if the enemy came, and take up their arms and take their places. If you want to imitate the Romans, you have to assign the making of the encampment to that company which you would want to put in the place of the Triari in the last part of the army.

But let us return to the discussion of the guards. I do not seem to find in connection with the ancients guarding the camp at night, that they had guards outside, distant from the ditches, as is the custom today, which they call the watch. I believe I should do this, when I think how the army could be easily deceived, because of the difficulty which exists in checking (reviewing) them, for they may be corrupted or attacked by the enemy, so that they judged it dangerous to trust them entirely or in part. And therefore all the power of their protection was within the ditches, which they dug with very great diligence and order, punishing capitally anyone who deviated from such an order. How this was arranged by them, I will not talk to you further in order not to tire you, since you are able to see it by yourselves, if you have not seen it up to now. I will say only briefly what would be done by me. I would regularly have a third of the army remain armed every night, and a fourth of them always on foot, who would be distributed throughout the embankments and all the places of the army, with double guards posted at each of its squares, where a part should remain, and a part continually go from one side of the encampment to the other. And this arrangement I describe, I would also observe by day if I had the enemy near. As to giving it a name, and renewing it every night, and doing the other things that are done in such guarding, since they are things (already) known, I will not talk further of them. I would only remind you of a most important matter, and by observing it do much good, by not observing it do much evil; which is, that great diligence be used as to who does not lodge within the camp at night, and who arrives there anew. And this is an easy matter, to review who is quartered there, with those arrangements we have designated, since every quarter having a predetermined number of men, it is an easy thing to see if there are any men missing or if any are left over; and when they are missing without permission, to punish them as fugitives, and if they are left over, to learn who they are, what they know, and what are their conditions. Such diligence results in the enemy not being able to have correspondence with your Heads, and not to have co-knowledge of your counsels. If this had not been observed with diligence by the Romans, Claudius Nero could not, when he had Hannibal near to him, have departed from the encampment he had in Lucania, and go and return from the Marches, without Hannibal having been aware of it. But it is not enough to make these good arrangements, unless they are made to be observed by great security, for there is nothing that wants so much observance as any required in the army. Therefore, the laws for their enforcement should be harsh and hard, and the executor very hard. The Romans punished with the capital penalty whoever was missing from the guard, whoever abandoned the place given him in combat, whoever brought anything concealed from outside the encampment; if anyone should tell of having performed some great act in battle, and should not have done it; if anyone should have fought except at the command of the Captain, if anyone from fear had thrown aside his arms. And if it occurred that an entire Cohort or an entire Legion had made a similar error, in order that they not all be put to death, they put their names in a purse, and drew the tenth part, and those they put to death. Which penalty was so carried out, that if everyone did not hear of it, they at least feared it. And because where there are severe punishments, there also ought to be rewards, so that men should fear and hope at the same time, they proposed rewards for every great deed; such as to him who, during the fighting, saved the life of one of its citizens, to whoever first climbed the walls of enemy towns, to whoever first entered the encampment of the enemy, to whoever in battle wounded or killed an enemy, to whoever had thrown him from his horse. And thus any act of virtue was recognized and rewarded by the Consuls, and publicly praised by everyone: and those who received gifts for any of these things, in addition to the glory and fame they acquired among the soldiers, when they returned to their country, exhibited them with solemn pomp and with great demonstrations among their friends and relatives. It is not to marvel therefore, if that people acquired so much empire, when they had so great an observance of punishment and reward toward them, which operated either for their good or evil, should merit either praise or censure; it behooves us to observe the greater part of these things. And it does not appear proper for me to be silent on a method of punishment observed by them, which was, that as the miscreant was convicted before the Tribune or the Consul, he was struck lightly by him with a rod: after which striking of the criminal, he was allowed to flee, and all the soldiers allowed to kill him, so that immediately each of them threw stones or darts, or hit him with other arms, of a kind from which he went little alive, and rarely returned to camp; and to such that did return to camp, he was not allowed to return home except with so much inconvenience and ignominy, that it was much better for him to die. You see this method almost observed by the Swiss, who have the condemned publicly put to death by the other soldiers. Which is well considered and done for the best, for if it is desired that one be not a defender of a criminal, the better remedy that is found, is to make him the punisher of him (the criminal); for in some respects he favors him while from other desires he longs for his punishment, if he himself is the executioner, than if the execution is carried out by another. If you want, therefore, that one is not to be favored in his mistakes by a people, a good remedy is to see to it that the public judge him. In support of this, the example of Manlius Capitol that can be cited, who, when he was accused by the Senate, was defended so much by the public up to the point where it no longer became the judge: but having become arbiter of his cause, condemned him to death. It is, therefore, a method of punishing this, of doing away with tumults, and of having justice observed. And since in restraining armed men, the fear of laws, or of men, is not enough, the ancients added the authority of God: and, therefore, with very great ceremony, they made their soldiers swear to observe the military discipline, so that if they did the contrary, they not only had to fear the laws and men, but God; and they used every industry to fill them with Religion.

Battista: Did the Romans permit women to be in their armies, or that they indulge in indolent games that are used to day?

Fabrizio: They prohibited both of them, and this prohibition was not very difficult, because the exercises which they gave each day to the soldiers were so many, sometimes being occupied all together, sometimes individually, that no time was left to them to think either of Venery, or of games, or of other things which make soldiers seditious and useless.

Battista: I like that. But tell me, when the army had to take off, what arrangements did they have?

Fabrizio: The captain's trumpet was sounded three times: at the first sound the tents were taken down and piled into heaps, at the second they loaded the burdens, and at the third they moved in the manner mentioned above, with the impedimenta behind, the armed men on every side, placing the Legions in the center. And, therefore, you would have to have a battalion of auxiliaries move, and behind it its particular impedimenta, and with those the fourth part of the public impedimenta, which would be all those who should be quartered in one of those (sections of the camp) which we showed a short while back. And, therefore, it would be well to have each one of them assigned to a battalion, so that when the army moved, everyone would know where his place was in marching. And every battalion ought to proceed on its way in this fashion with its own impedimenta, and with a quarter of the public (impedimenta) at its rear, as we showed the Roman army marched.

Battista: In placing the encampment, did they have other considerations than those you mentioned?

Fabrizio: I tell you again, that in their encampments, the Romans wanted to be able to employ the usual form of their method, in the observance of which, they took no other consideration. But as to other considerations, they had two principal ones: the one, to locate themselves in a healthy place: the other to locate themselves where the enemy should be unable to besiege them, and cut off their supply of water and provisions. To avoid this weakness, therefore, they avoided marshy places, or exposure to noxious winds. They recognized these, not so much from the characteristics of the site, but from the looks of the inhabitants: and if they saw them with poor color, or short winded, or full of other infections, they did not encamp there. As to the other part of not being besieged, the nature of the place must be considered, where the friends are, and where the enemy, and from these make a conjecture whether or not you can be besieged. And, therefore, the Captain must be very expert concerning sites of the countries, and have around him many others who have the same expertness. They also avoided sickness and hunger so as not to disorganize the army; for if you want to keep it healthy, you must see to it that the soldiers sleep under tents, that they are quartered, where there are trees to create shade, where there is wood to cook the food, and not to march in the heat. You need, therefore, to consider the encampment the day before you arrive there, and in winter guard against marching in the snow and through ice without the convenience of making a fire, and not lack necessary clothing, and not to drink bad water. Those who get sick in the house, have them taken care of by doctors; for a captain has no remedy when he has to fight both sickness and the enemy. But nothing is more useful in maintaining an army healthy than exercise: and therefore the ancients made them exercise every day. Whence it is seen how much exercise is of value, for in the quarters it keeps you healthy, and in battle it makes you victorious. As to hunger, not only is it necessary to see that the enemy does not impede your provisions, but to provide whence you are to obtain them, and to see that those you have are not lost. And, therefore, you must always have provisions (on hand) for the army for a month, and beyond that to tax the neighboring friends that they provide you daily, keep the provisions in a strong place, and, above all, dispense it with diligence, giving each one a reasonable measure each day, and so observe this part that they do not become disorganized; for every other thing in war can be overcome with time, this only with time overcomes you. Never make anyone your enemy, who, while seeking to overcome you with the sword (iron), can overcome you by hunger, because if such a victory is not as honorable, it is more secure and more certain. That army, therefore, cannot escape hunger which does not observe justice, and licentiously consume whatever it please, for one evil causes the provisions not to arrive, and the other that when they arrive, they are uselessly consumed: therefore the ancients arranged that what was given was eaten, and in the time they assigned, so that no soldier ate except when the Captain did. Which, as to being observed by the modern armies, everyone does (the contrary), and deservedly they cannot be called orderly and sober as the ancients, but licentious and drunkards.

Battista: You have said in the beginning of arranging the encampment, that you did not want to stay only with two battalions, but took up four, to show how a fair (sized) army was quartered. Therefore I would want you to tell me two things: the one, if I have more or less men, how should I quarter them: the other, what number of soldiers would be enough to fight against any enemy?

Fabrizio: To the first question, I reply, that if the army has four or six thousand soldiers more or less, rows of quarters are taken away or added as are needed, and in this way it is possible to accommodate more or fewer infinitely. nonetheless, when the Romans joined together two consular armies, they made two encampments and had the parts of the disarmed men face each other. As to the second question, I reply, that the regular Roman army had about twenty four thousand soldiers: but when a great force pressed them, the most they assembled were fifty thousand. With this number they opposed two hundred thousand Gauls whom they assaulted after the first war which they had with the Carthaginians. With the same number, they opposed Hannibal. And you have to note that the Romans and Greeks had made war with few (soldiers), strengthened by order and by art; the westerners and easterners had made it with a multitude: but one of these nations serves itself of natural fury, as are the westerners; the other of the great obedience which its men show to their King. But in Greece and Italy, as there is not this natural fury, nor the natural reverence toward their King, it has been necessary to turn to discipline; which is so powerful, that it made the few able to overcome the fury and natural obstinacy of the many. I tell you, therefore, if you want to imitate the Romans and Greeks, the number of fifty thousand soldiers ought not to be exceeded, rather they should actually be less; for the many cause confusion, and do not allow discipline to be observed nor the orders learned. And Pyrrhus used to say that with fifteen thousand men he would assail the world.

But let us pass on to another part. We have made our army win an engagement, and I showed the troubles that can occur in battle; we have made it march, and I have narrated with what impedimenta it can be surrounded while marching: and lastly we have quartered it: where not only a little repose from past hardship ought to be taken, but also to think about how the war ought to be concluded; for in the quarters, many things are discussed, especially if there remain enemies in the field, towns under suspicion, of which it is well to reassure oneself, and to capture those which are hostile. It is necessary, therefore, to come to these demonstrations, and to pass over this difficulty with that (same) glory with which we have fought up to the present. Coming down to particulars, therefore, that if it should happen to you that many men or many peoples should do something, which might be useful to you and very harmful to them, as would be the destruction of the walls of their City, or the sending of many of themselves into exile, it is necessary that you either deceive them in a way that everyone should believe he is affected, so that one not helping the other, all find themselves oppressed without a remedy, or rather, to command everyone what they ought to do on the same day, so that each one believing himself to be alone to whom the command is given, thinks of obeying it, and not of a remedy; and thus, without tumult, your command is executed by everyone. If you should have suspicion of the loyalty of any people, and should want to assure yourself and occupy them without notice, in order to disguise your design more easily, you cannot do better than to communicate to him some of your design, requesting his aid, and indicate to him you want to undertake another enterprise, and to have a mind alien to every thought of his: which will cause him not to think of his defense, as he does not believe you are thinking of attacking him, and he will give you the opportunity which will enable you to satisfy your desire easily. If you should have present in your army someone who keeps the enemy advised of your designs, you cannot do better if you want to avail yourself of his evil intentions, than to communicate to him those things you do not want to do, and keep silent those things you want to do, and tell him you are apprehensive of the things of which you are not apprehensive, and conceal those things of which you are apprehensive: which will cause the enemy to undertake some enterprise, in the belief that he knows your designs, in which you can deceive him and defeat him. If you should design [as did Claudius Nero] to decrease your army, sending aid to some friend, and they should not be aware of it, it is necessary that the encampment be not decreased, but to maintain entire all the signs and arrangements, making the same fires and posting the same guards as for the entire army. Likewise, if you should attach a new force to your army, and do not want the enemy to know you have enlarged it, it is necessary that the encampment be not increased, for it is always most useful to keep your designs secret. Whence Metellus, when he was with the armies in Spain, to one who asked him what he was going to do the next day, answered that if his shirt knew it, he would burn it. Marcus Crassus, to one who asked him when he was going to move his army, said: "do you believe you are alone in not hearing the trumpets?" If you should desire to learn the secrets of your enemy and know his arrangement, some used to send ambassadors, and with them men expert in war disguised in the clothing of the family, who, taking the opportunity to observe the enemy army, and consideration of his strengths and weaknesses, have given them the occasion to defeat him. Some have sent a close friend of theirs into exile, and through him have learned the designs of their adversary. You may also learn similar secrets from the enemy if you should take prisoners for this purpose. Marius, in the war he waged against Cimbri, in order to learn the loyalty of those Gauls who lived in Lombardy and were leagued with the Roman people, sent them letters, open and sealed: and in the open ones he wrote them that they should not open the sealed ones except at such a time: and before that time, he called for them to be returned, and finding them opened, knew their loyalty was not complete.

Some Captains, when they were assaulted have not wanted to go to meet the enemy, but have gone to assail his country, and constrain him to return to defend his home. This often has turned out well, because your soldiers begin to win and fill themselves with booty and confidence, while those of the enemy become dismayed, it appearing to them that from being winners, they have become losers. So that to whoever has made this diversion, it has turned out well. But this can only be done by that man who has his country stronger than that of the enemy, for if it were otherwise, he would go on to lose. It has often been a useful thing for a Captain who finds himself besieged in the quarters of the enemy, to set in motion proceedings for an accord, and to make a truce with him for several days; which only an enemy negligent in every way will do, so that availing yourself of his negligence, you can easily obtain the opportunity to get out of his hands. Sulla twice freed himself from his enemies in this manner, and with this same deceit, Hannibal in Spain got away from the forces of Claudius Nero, who had besieged him.

It also helps one in freeing himself from the enemy to do something in addition to those mentioned, which keeps him at bay. This is done in two ways: either by assaulting him with part of your forces, so that intent on the battle, he gives the rest of your forces the opportunity to be able to save themselves, or to have some new incident spring up, which, by the novelty of the thing, makes him wonder, and for this reason to become apprehensive and stand still, as you know Hannibal did, who, being trapped by Fabius Maximus, at night placed some torches between the horns of many oxen, so that Fabius in suspense over this novelty, did not think further of impeding his passage. A Captain ought, among all the other actions of his, endeavor with every art to divide the forces of the enemy, either by making him suspicious of his men in whom he trusted, or by giving him cause that he has to separate his forces, and, because of this, become weaker. The first method is accomplished by watching the things of some of those whom he has next to him, as exists in war, to save his possessions, maintaining his children or other of his necessities without charge. You know how Hannibal, having burned all the fields around Rome, caused only those of Fabius Maximus to remain safe. You know how Coriolanus, when he came with the army to Rome, saved the possessions of the Nobles, and burned and sacked those of the Plebs. When Metellus led the army against Jugurtha, all the ambassadors, sent to him by Jugurtha, were requested by him to give up Jugurtha as a prisoner; afterwards, writing letters to these same people on the same subject, wrote in such a way that in a little while Jugurtha became suspicious of all his counsellors, and in different ways, dismissed them. Hannibal, having taken refuge with Antiochus, the Roman ambassadors frequented him so much at home, that Antiochus becoming suspicious of him, did not afterwards have any faith in his counsels. As to dividing the enemy forces, there is no more certain way than to have one country assaulted by part of them (your forces), so that being constrained to go to defend it, they (of that country) abandon the war. This is the method employed by Fabius when his Army had encountered the forces of the Gauls, the Tuscans, Umbrians, and Samnites. Titus Didius, having a small force in comparison with those of the enemy, and awaiting a Legion from Rome, the enemy wanted to go out to meet it; so that in order that it should not do so, he gave out by voice throughout his army that he wanted to undertake an engagement with the enemy on the next day; then he took steps that some of the prisoners he had were given the opportunity to escape, who carried back the order of the Consul to fight on the next day, (and) caused the enemy, in order not to diminish his forces, not to go out to meet that Legion: and in this way, kept himself safe. Which method did not serve to divide the forces of the enemy, but to double his own. Some, in order to divide his (the enemy) forces, have employed allowing him to enter their country, and (in proof) allowed him to take many towns so that by placing guards in them, he diminished his forces, and in this manner having made him weak, assaulted and defeated him. Some others, when they wanted to go into one province, feigned making an assault on another, and used so much industry, that as soon as they extended toward that one where there was no fear they would enter, have overcome it before the enemy had time to succor it. For the enemy, as he is not certain whether you are to return back to the place first threatened by you, is constrained not to abandon the one place and succor the other, and thus often he does not defend either.

In addition to the matters mentioned, it is important to a Captain when sedition or discord arises among the soldiers, to know how to extinguish it with art. The better way is to castigate the heads of this folly (error); but to do it in a way that you are able to punish them before they are able to become aware of it. The method is, if they are far from you, not to call only the guilty ones, but all the others together with them, so that as they do not believe there is any cause to punish them, they are not disobedient, but provide the opportunity for punishment. When they are present, one ought to strengthen himself with the guiltless, and by their aid, punish them. If there should be discord among them, the best way is to expose them to danger, which fear will always make them united. But, above all, what keeps the Army united, is the reputation of its Captain, which only results from his virtue, for neither blood (birth) or authority attain it without virtue. And the first thing a Captain is expected to do, is to see to it that the soldiers are paid and punished; for any time payment is missed, punishment must also be dispensed with, because you cannot castigate a soldier you rob, unless you pay him; and as he wants to live, he can abstain from being robbed. But if you pay him but do not punish him, he becomes insolent in every way, because you become of little esteem, and to whomever it happens, he cannot maintain the dignity of his position; and if he does not maintain it, of necessity, tumults and discords follow, which are the ruin of an Army. The Ancient Captains had a molestation from which the present ones are almost free, which was the interpretation of sinister omen to their undertakings; for if an arrow fell in an army, if the Sun or the Moon was obscured, if an earthquake occurred, if the Captain fell while either mounting or dismounting from his horse, it was interpreted in a sinister fashion by the soldiers, and instilled so much fear in them, that when they came to an engagement, they were easily defeated. And, therefore, as soon as such an incident occurred, the ancient Captains either demonstrated the cause of it or reduced it to its natural causes, or interpreted it to (favor) their own purposes. When Caesar went to Africa, and having fallen while he was putting out to sea, said, "Africa, I have taken you:" and many have profited from an eclipse of the Moon and from earthquakes: these things cannot happen in our time, as much because our men are not as super-stitious, as because our Religion, by itself, entirely takes away such ideas. Yet if it should occur, the orders of the ancients should be imitated.

When, either from hunger, or other natural necessity, or human passion, your enemy is brought to extreme desperation, and, driven by it, comes to fight with you, you ought to remain within your quarters, and avoid battle as much as you can. Thus the Lacedemonians did against the Messinians: thus Caesar did against Afranius and Petreius. When Fulvius was Consul against the Cimbri, he had the cavalry assault the enemy continually for many days, and considered how they would issue forth from their quarters in order to pursue them; whence he placed an ambush behind the quarters of the Cimbri, and had them assaulted by the cavalry, and when the Cimbri came out of their quarters to pursue them, Fulvius seized them and plundered them. It has been very effective for a Captain, when his army is in the vicinity of the enemy army, to send his forces with the insignia of the enemy, to rob and burn his own country: whence the enemy, believing they were forces coming to their aid, also ran out to help them plunder, and, because of this, have become disorganized and given the adversary the faculty of overcoming them. Alexander of Epirus used these means fighting against the Illirici, and Leptenus the Syracusan against the Carthaginians, and the design succeeded happily for both. Many have overcome the enemy by giving him the faculty of eating and drinking beyond his means, feigning being afraid, and leaving his quarters full of wine and herds, and when the enemy had filled himself beyond every natural limit, they assaulted him and overcome him with injury to him. Thus Tamirus did against Cyrus, and Tiberius Gracchus against the Spaniards. Some have poisoned the wine and other things to eat in order to be able to overcome them more easily. A little while ago, I said I did not find the ancients had kept a night watch outside, and I thought they did it to avoid the evils that could happen, for it has been found that sometimes, the sentries posted in the daytime to keep watch for the enemy, have been the ruin of him who posted them; for it has happened often that when they had been taken, and by force had been made to give the signal by which they called their own men, who, coming at the signal, have been either killed or taken.

Sometimes it helps to deceive the enemy by changing one of your habits, relying on which, he is ruined: as a Captain had already done, who, when he wanted to have a signal made to his men indicating the coming of the enemy, at night with fire and in the daytime with smoke, commanded that both smoke and flame be made without any intermission; so that when the enemy came, he should remain in the belief that he came without being seen, as he did not see the signals (usually) made to indicate his discovery, made [because of his going disorganized] the victory of his adversary easier. Menno Rodius, when he wanted to draw the enemy from the strong places, sent one in the disguise of a fugitive, who affirmed that his army was full of discord, and that the greater part were deserting, and to give proof of the matter, had certain tumults started among the quarters: whence the enemy, thinking he was able to break him, assaulted him and was routed.

In addition to the things mentioned, one ought to take care not to bring the enemy to extreme desperation; which Caesar did when he fought the Germans, who, having blocked the way to them, seeing that they were unable to flee, and necessity having made them brave, desired rather to undergo the hardship of pursuing them if they defended themselves. Lucullus, when he saw that some Macedonian cavalry who were with him, had gone over to the side of the enemy, quickly sounded the call to battle, and commanded the other forces to pursue it: whence the enemy, believing that Lucullus did not want to start the battle, went to attack the Macedonians with such fury, that they were constrained to defend themselves, and thus, against their will, they became fighters of the fugitives. Knowing how to make yourself secure of a town when you have doubts of its loyalty once you have conquered it, or before, is also important; which some examples of the ancients teach you. Pompey, when he had doubts of the Catanians, begged them to accept some infirm people he had in his army, and having sent some very robust men in the disguise of infirm ones, occupied the town. Publius Valerius, fearful of the loyalty of the Epidaurians, announced an amnesty to be held, as we will tell you, at a Church outside the town, and when all the public had gone there for the amnesty, he locked the doors, and then let no one out from inside except those whom he trusted. Alexander the Great, when he wanted to go into Asia and secure Thrace for himself, took with him all the chiefs of this province, giving them provisions, and placed lowborn men in charge of the common people of Thrace; and thus he kept the chiefs content by paying them, and the common people quiet by not having Heads who should disquiet them. But among all the things by which Captains gain the people over to themselves, are the examples of chastity and justice, as was that of Scipio in Spain when he returned that girl, beautiful in body, to her husband and father, which did more than arms in gaining over Spain. Caesar, when he paid for the lumber that he used to make the stockades around his army in Gaul, gained such a name for himself of being just, that he facilitated the acquisition of that province for himself. I do not know what else remains for me to talk about regarding such events, and there does not remain any part of this matter that has not been discussed by us. The only thing lacking is to tell of the methods of capturing and defending towns, which I am about to do willingly, if it is not painful for you now.

Battista: Your humaneness is so great, that it makes us pursue our desires without being afraid of being held presumptuous, since you have offered it willingly, that we would be ashamed to ask you. Therefore we say only this to you, that you cannot do a greater or more thankful benefit to us than to furnish us this discussion. But before you pass on to that other matter, resolve a doubt for us: whether it is better to continue the war even in winter, as is done today, or wage it only in the summer, and go into quarters in the winter, as the ancients did.

Fabrizio: Here, if there had not been the prudence of the questioner, some part that merits consideration would have been omitted. I tell you again that the ancients did everything better and with more prudence than we; and if some error is made in other things, all are made in matters of war. There is nothing more imprudent or more perilous to a Captain than to wage war in winter, and more dangerous to him who brings it, than to him who awaits it. The reason is this: all the industry used in military discipline, is used in order to be organized to undertake an engagement with your enemy, as this is the end toward which a Captain must aim, for the engagement makes you win or lose a war. Therefore, whoever knows how to organize it better, and who has his army better disciplined, has the greater advantage in this, and can hope more to win it. On the other hand, there is nothing more inimical to organization than the rough sides, or cold and wet seasons; for the rough side does not allow you to use the plentitude (of your forces) according to discipline, and the cold and wet seasons do not allow you to keep your forces together, and you cannot have them face the enemy united, but of necessity, you must quarter them separately, and without order, having to take into account the castles, hamlets, and farm houses that receive you; so that all the hard work employed by you in disciplining your army is in vain. And do not marvel if they war in winter time today, for as the armies are without discipline, and do not know the harm that is done to them by not being quartered together, for their annoyance does not enable those arrangements to be made and to observe that discipline which they do not have. Yet, the injury caused by campaigning in the field in the winter ought to be observed, remembering that the French in the year one thousand five hundred three (1503) were routed on the Garigliano by the winter, and not by the Spaniards. For, as I have told you, whoever assaults has even greater disadvantage, because weather harms him more when he is in the territory of others, and wants to make war. Whence he is compelled either to withstand the inconveniences of water and cold in order to keep together, or to divide his forces to escape them. But whoever waits, can select the place to his liking, and await him (the enemy) with fresh forces, and can unite them in a moment, and go out to find the enemy forces who cannot withstand their fury. Thus were the French routed, and thus are those always routed who assault an enemy in winter time, who in itself has prudence. Whoever, therefore, does not want the forces, organization, discipline, and virtue, in some part, to be of value, makes war in the field in the winter time. And because the Romans wanted to avail themselves of all of these things, into which they put so much industry, avoided not only the winter time, but rough mountains and difficult places, and anything else which could impede their ability to demonstrate their skill and virtue. So this suffices to (answer) your question; and now let us come to treat of the attacking and defending of towns, and of the sites, and of their edifices.

SEVENTH BOOK

You ought to know that towns and fortresses can be strong either by nature or industry. Those are strong by nature which are surrounded by rivers or marshes, as is Mantua or Ferrara, or those situated on a rock or sloping mountain, as Monaco and San Leo; for those situated on mountains which are not difficult to climb, today are [with respect to caves and artillery] very weak. And, therefore, very often today a plain is sought on which to build (a city) to make it strong by industry. The first industry is, to make the walls twisted and full of turned recesses; which pattern results in the enemy not being able to approach them, as they will be able to be attacked easily not only from the front, but on the flanks. If the walls are made too high, they are excessively exposed to the blows of the artillery; if they are made too low, they are very easily scaled. If you dig ditches (moats) in front of them to make it difficult (to employ) ladders, if it should happen that the enemy fills them [which a large army can do easily] the wall becomes prey to the enemy. I believe, therefore, [subject to a better judgement] that if you want to make provision against both evils the wall ought to be made high, with the ditches inside and not outside. This is the strongest way to build that is possible, for it protects you from artillery and ladders, and does not give the enemy the faculty of filling the ditches. The wall, therefore, ought to be as high as occurs to you, and not less than three arm lengths wide, to make it more difficult to be ruined. It ought to have towers placed at intervals of two hundred arm lengths. The ditch inside ought to be at least thirty arm lengths wide and twelve deep, and all the

146

earth that is excavated in making the ditch is thrown toward the city, and is sustained by a wall that is part of the base of the ditch, and extends again as much above the ground, as that a man may take cover behind it: which has the effect of making the depth of the ditch greater. In the base of the ditch, every two hundred arm lengths, there should be a matted enclosure, which with the artillery, causes injury to anyone who should descend into it. The heavy artillery which defends the city, are placed behind the wall enclosing the ditch; for to defend the wall from the front, as it is high, it is not possible to use conveniently anything else other than small or middle sized guns. If the enemy comes to scale your wall, the height of the first wall easily protects you. If he comes with artillery, he must first batter down the first wall: but once it is battered down, because the nature of all batterings is to cause the wall to fall toward the battered side, the ruin of the wall will result [since it does not find a ditch which receives and hides it] in doubling the depth of the ditch, so that it is not possible for you to pass on further as you will find a ruin that holds you back and a ditch which will impede you, and from the wall of the ditch, in safety, the enemy artillery kills you. The only remedy there exists for you, is to fill up the ditch: which is very difficult, as much because its capacity is large, as from the difficulty you have in approaching it, since the walls being winding and recessed, you can enter among them only with difficulty, for the reasons previously mentioned; and then, having to climb over the ruin with the material in hand, causes you a very great difficulty: so that I know a city so organized is completely indestructible.

Battista: If, in addition to the ditch inside, there should be one also on the outside, wouldn't (the encampment) be stronger?

Fabrizio: It would be, without doubt; but my reasoning is, that if you want to dig one ditch only, it is better inside than outside.

Battista: Would you have water in the ditch, or would you leave them dry?

Fabrizio: Opinions are different; for ditches full of water protect you from (subterranean) tunnels, the ditches without water make it more difficult for you to fill them in again. But, considering everything, I would have them without water; for they are more secure, and, as it has been observed that in winter time the ditches ice over, the capture of a city is made easy, as happened at Mirandola when Pope Julius besieged it. And to protect yourself from tunnels, I would dig them so deep, that whoever should want to go (tunnel) deeper, should find water. I would also build the fortresses in a way similar to the walls and ditches, so that similar difficulty would be encountered in destroying it. I want to call to mind one good thing to anyone who defends a city. This is, that they do not erect bastions outside, and they be distant from its wall. And another to anyone who builds the fortresses: And this is, that he not build any redoubts in them, into which whoever is inside can retire when the wall is lost. What makes me give the first counsel is, that no one ought to do anything, through the medium of which, you begin to lose your reputation without any remedy, the loss of which makes others esteem you less, and dismay those who undertake your defense. And what I say will always happen to you if you erect bastions outside the town you have to defend, for you will always lose them, as you are unable to defend small things when they are placed under the fury of the artillery; so that in losing them, they become the beginning and the cause of your ruin. Genoa, when it rebelled from King Louis of France, erected some bastions on the hills outside the City, which, as soon as they were lost, and they were lost quickly, also caused the city to be lost. As to the second counsel, I affirm there is nothing more dangerous concerning a fortress, than to be able to retire into it, for the hope that men have (lose) when they abandon a place, cause it to be lost, and when it is lost, it then causes the entire fortress to be lost. For an example, there is the recent loss of the fortress of Forli when the Countess Catherine defended it against Cesare Borgia, son of Pope Alexander the Sixth, who had led the army of the King of France. That entire fortress was full of places by both of them: For it was originally a citadel. There was a moat before coming to the fortress, so that it was entered by means of a draw bridge. The fortress was divided into three parts, and each part separated by a ditch, and with water between them; and one passed from one place to another by means of bridges: whence the Duke battered one of those parts of the fortress with artillery, and opened up part of a wall; whence Messer Giovanni Da Casale, who was in charge of the garrison, did not think of defending that opening, but abandoned to retire into the other places; so that the forces of the Duke, having entered that part without opposition, immediately seized all of it, for they became masters of the bridges that connected the members (parts) with each other. He lost the fort which was held to be indestructible because of two mistakes: one, because it had so many redoubts: the other, because no one was made master of his bridges (they were unprotected). The poorly built fortress and the little prudence of the defender, therefore, brought disgrace to the magnanimous enterprise of the Countess, who had the courage to face an army which neither the King of Naples, nor the Duke of Milan, had faced. And although his (the Duke) efforts did not have a good ending, nonetheless, he became noted for those honors which his virtue merited. Which was testified to by the many epigrams made in those times praising him. If I should therefore have to build a fortress, I would make its walls strong, and ditches in the manner we have discussed, nor would I build anything else to live in but houses, and they would be weak and low, so that they would not impede the sight of the walls to anyone who might be in the plaza, so that the Captain should be able to see with (his own) eyes where he could be of help, and that everyone should understand that if the walls and the ditch were lost, the entire fortress would be lost. And even if I should build some redoubts, I would have the bridges so separated, that each part should be master of (protect) the bridge in its own area, arranging that it be buttressed on its pilasters in the middle of the ditch.

Battista: You have said that, today, the little things cannot be defended, and it seems to me I have understood the opposite, that the smaller the thing was, the better it was defended.

Fabrizio: You have not understood well, for today that place cannot be called strong, where he who defends it does not have room to retire among new ditches and ramparts: for such is the fury of the artillery, that he who relies on the protection of only one wall or rampart, deceives himself. And as the bastions [if you want them not to exceed their regular measurements, for then they would be terraces and castles] are not made so that others can retire into them, they are lost quickly. And therefore it is a wise practice to leave these bastions outside, and fortify the entrances of the terraces, and cover their gates with revets, so that one does not go in or out of the gate in a straight line, and there is a ditch with a bridge over it from the revet to the gate. The gates are also fortified with shutters, so as to allow your men to reenter, when, after going out to fight, it happens that the enemy drives them back, and in the ensuing mixing of men, the enemy does not enter with them. And therefore, these things have also been found which the ancients called "cataracts," which, being let down, keep out the enemy but save one's friends; for in such cases, one cannot avail himself of anything else, neither bridges, or the gate, since both are occupied by the crowd.

Battista: I have seen these shutters that you mention, made of small beams, in Germany, in the form of iron grids, while those of ours are made entirely of massive planks. I would want to know whence this difference arises, and which is stronger.

Fabrizio: I will tell you again, that the methods and organizations of war in all the world, with respect to those of the ancients, are extinct; but in Italy, they are entirely lost, and if there is something more powerful, it results from the examples of the Ultramontanes. You may have heard, and these others can remember, how weakly things were built before King Charles of France crossed into Italy in the year one thousand four hundred ninety four (1494). The battlements were made a half arm length thin (wide), the places for the cross-bowmen and bombardiers (gunners) were made with a small aperture outside and a large one inside, and with many other defects, which I will omit, not to be tedious; for the defenses are easily taken away from slender battlements; the (places for) bombardiers built that way are easily opened (demolished). Now from the French, we have learned to make the battlements wide and large, and also to make the (places of the) bombardiers wide on the inside, and narrow it at the center of the wall, and then again widen it up to the outside edge: and this results in the artillery being able to demolish its defenses only with difficulty, The French, moreover, have many other arrangements such as these, which, because they have not been seen thus, have not been given consideration. Among which, is this method of the shutters made in the form of a grid, which is by far a better method than yours; for if you have to repair the shutters of a gate such as yours, lowering it if you are locked inside, and hence are unable to injure the enemy, so that they can attack it safely either in the dark or with a fire. But if it is made in the shape of a grid, you can, once it is lowered, by those weaves and intervals, be able to defend it with lances, cross-bows, and every other kind of arms.

Battista: I have also seen another Ultramontane custom in Italy, and it is this, making the carriages of the artillery with the spokes of the wheels bent toward the axles. I would like to know why they make them this way, as it seems to me they would be stronger straight, as those of our wheels.

Fabrizio: Never believe that things which differ from the ordinary are made at home, but if you would believe that I should make them such as to be more beautiful, you would err; for where strength is necessary, no account is taken of beauty; but they all arise from being safer and stronger than ours. The reason is this. When the carriage is loaded, it either goes on a level, or inclines to the right or left side. When it goes level, the wheels equally sustain the weight, which, being divided equally between them, does not burden them much; when it inclines, it comes to have all the weight of the load upon that wheel on which it inclines. If its spokes are straight, they can easily collapse, since the wheel being inclined, the spokes also come to incline, and do not sustain the weight in a straight line. And, thus, when the carriage rides level and when they carry less weight, they come to be stronger; when the carriage rides inclined and when they carry more weight, they are weaker. The contrary happens to the bent spokes of the French carriages; for when the carriage inclines to one side, it points (leans straight) on them, since being ordinarily bent, they then come to be (more) straight (vertical), and can sustain all the weight strongly; and when the carriage goes level and they (the spokes) are bent, they sustain half the weight.

But let us return to our Cities and Fortresses. The French, for the greater security of their towns, and to enable them during sieges to put into and withdraw forces from them more easily, also employ, in addition to the things mentioned, another arrangement, of which I have not yet seen any example in Italy: and it is this, that they erect two pilasters at the outside point of a draw-bridge, and upon each of them they balance a beam so that half of it comes over the bridge, and the other half outside. Then they join small beams to the part outside, which are woven together from one beam to another in the shape of a grid, and on the inside they attach a chain to the end of each beam. When they want to close the bridge from the outside, therefore, they release the chains and allow all that gridded part to drop, which closes the bridge when it is lowered, and when they want to open it, they pull on the chains, and they (gridded beams) come to be raised; and they can be raised so that a man can pass under, but not a horse, and also so much that a horse with the man can pass under, and also can be closed entirely, for it is lowered and raised like a lace curtain. This arrangement is more secure than the shutters: for it can be impeded by the enemy so that it can come down only with difficulty, (and) it does not come down in a straight line like the shutters which can easily be penetrated. Those who want to build a City, therefore, ought to have all the things mentioned installed; and in addition, they should want at least one mile around the wall where either farming or building would not be allowed, but should be open field where no bushes, embankments, trees, or houses, should exist which would impede the vision, and which should be in the rear of a besieging enemy. It is to be noted that a town which has its ditches outside with its embankments higher than the ground, is very weak; for they provide a refuge for the enemy who assaults you, but does not impede him in attacking you, because they can be easily forced (opened) and give his artillery an emplacement.

But let us pass into the town. I do not want to waste much time in showing you that, in addition to the things mentioned previously, provisions for living and fighting supplies must also be included, for they are the things which everyone needs, and without them, every other provision is in vain. And, generally, two things ought to be done, provision yourself, and deprive the enemy of the opportunity to avail himself of the resources of your country. Therefore, any straw, grain, and cattle, which you cannot receive in your house, ought to be destroyed. Whoever defends a town ought to see to it that nothing is done in a tumultuous and disorganized manner, and have means to let everyone know what he has to do in any incident. The manner is this, that the women, children, aged, and the public stay at home, and leave the town free to the young and the brave: who armed, are distributed for defense, part being on the walls, part at the gates, part in the principal places of the City, in order to remedy those evils which might arise within; another part is not assigned to any place, but is prepared to help anyone requesting their help. And when matters are so organized, only with difficulty can tumults arise which disturb you. I want you to note also that in attacking and defending Cities, nothing gives the enemy hope of being able to occupy a town, than to know the inhabitants are not in the habit of looking for the enemy; for often Cities are lost entirely from fear, without any other action. When one assaults such a City, he should make all his appearances (ostentatious) terrible. On the other hand, he who is assaulted ought to place brave men, who are not afraid of thoughts, but by arms, on the side where the enemy (comes to) fight; for if the attempt proves vain, courage grows in the besieged, and then the enemy is forced to overcome those inside with his virtue and his reputation.

The equipment with which the ancients defended the towns were many, such as, Ballistas, Onagers, Scorpions, Arc-Ballistas, Large Bows, Slingshots; and those with which they assaulted were also many, such as, Battering Rams, Wagons, Hollow Metal Fuses (Muscoli), Trench Covers (Plutei), Siege Machines (Vinee), Scythes, Turtles (somewhat similar to present day tanks). In place of these things, today there is the artillery, which serves both attackers and defenders, and, hence, I will not speak further about it. But let us return to our discussion, and come to the details of the siege (attack). One ought to take care not to be able to be taken by hunger, and not to be forced (to capitulate) by assaults. As to hunger, it has been said that it is necessary, before the siege arrives, to be well provided with food. But when it is lacking during a long siege, some extraordinary means of being provided by friends who want to save you, have been observed to be employed, especially if a river runs in the middle of the besieged City, as were the Romans, when their castle of Casalino was besieged by Hannibal, who, not being able to send them anything else by way of the river, threw great quantities of nuts into it, which being carried by the river without being able to be impeded, fed the Casalinese for some time. Some, when they were besieged, in order to show the enemy they had grain left over, and to make them despair of being able to besiege (defeat) them by hunger, have either thrown bread outside the walls, or have given a calf grain to eat, and then allowed it to be taken, so that when it was killed, and being found full of grain, gave signs of an abundance which they do not have. On the other hand, excellent Captains have used various methods to enfamish the enemy. Fabius allowed the Campanians to sow so that they should lack that grain which they were sowing. Dionysius, when he was besieged at Reggio, feigned wanting to make an accord with them, and while it was being drawn, had himself provided with food, and then when, by this method, had depleted them of grain, pressed them and starved them. Alexander the Great, when he wanted to capture Leucadia, captured all the surrounding castles, and allowed the men from them to take refuge in it (the City), and thus by adding a great multitude, he starved them.

As to assaults, it has been said that one ought to guard against the first onrush, with which the Romans often occupied many towns, assaulting them all at once from every side, and they called it attacking the city by its crown: as did Scipio when he occupied new Carthage in Spain. If this onrush is withstood, then only with difficulty will you be overcome. And even if it should occur that the enemy had entered inside the city by having forced the walls, even the small terraces give you some remedy if they are not abandoned; for many armies have, once they have entered into a town, been repulsed or slain. The remedy is, that the townspeople keep themselves in high places, and fight them from their houses and towers. Which thing, those who have entered in the City, have endeavored to win in two ways: the one, to open the gates of the City and make a way for the townspeople by which they can escape in safety: the other, to send out a (message) by voice signifying that no one would be harmed unless armed, and whoever would throw his arms on the ground, they would pardon. Which thing has made the winning of many Cities easy. In addition to this, Cities are easy to capture if you fall on them unexpectedly, which you can do when you find yourself with your army far away, so that they do not believe that you either want to assault them, or that you can do it without your presenting yourself, because of the distance from the place. Whence, if you assault them secretly and quickly, it will almost always happen that you will succeed in reporting the victory. I unwillingly discuss those things which have happened in our times, as I would burden you with myself and my (ideas), and I would not know what to say in discussing other things. nonetheless, concerning this matter, I cannot but cite the example of Cesare Borgia, called the Duke Valentine, who, when he was at Nocera with his forces, under the pretext of going to harm Camerino, turned toward the State of Urbino, and occupied a State in one day and without effort, which some other, with great time and expense, would barely have occupied.

Those who are besieged must also guard themselves from the deceit and cunning of the enemy, and, therefore, the besieged should not trust anything which they see the enemy doing continuously, but always believe they are being done by deceit, and can change to injure them. When Domitius Calvinus was besieging a town, he undertook habitually to circle the walls of the City every day with a good part of his forces. Whence the townspeople, believing he was doing this for exercise, lightened the guard: when Domitius became aware of this, he assaulted them, and destroyed them. Some Captains, when they heard beforehand that aid was to come to the besieged, have clothed their soldiers with the insignia of those who were to come, and having introduced them inside, have occupied the town.

Chimon, the Athenian, one night set fire to a Temple that was outside the town, whence, when the townspeople arrived to succor it, they left the town to the enemy to plunder. Some have put to death those who left the besieged castle to blacksmith (shoe horses), and redressing their soldiers with the clothes of the blacksmiths, who then surrendered the town to him. The ancient Captains also employed various methods to despoil the garrisons of the towns they want to take. Scipio, when he was in Africa, and desiring to occupy several castles in which garrisons had been placed by Carthaginians, feigned several times wanting to assault them, but then from fear not only abstained, but drew away from them. Which Hannibal believing to be true, in order to pursue him with a larger force and be able to attack him more easily, withdrew all the garrisons from them: (and) Scipio becoming aware of this, sent Maximus, his Captain, to capture them. Pyrrhus, when he was waging war in Sclavonia, in one of the Chief Cities of that country, where a large force had been brought in to garrison it, feigned to be desperate of being able to capture it, and turning to other places, caused her, in order to succor them, to empty herself of the garrison, so that it became easy to be forced (captured). Many have polluted the water and diverted rivers to take a town, even though they then did not succeed. Sieges and surrenders are also easily accomplished, by dismaying them by pointing out an accomplished victory, or new help which is come to their disfavor. The ancient Captains sought to occupy towns by treachery, corrupting some inside, but have used different methods. Some have sent one of their men under the disguise of a fugitive, who gained authority and confidence with the enemy, which he afterward used for his own benefit. Many by this means have learned the procedures of the guards, and through this knowledge have taken the town. Some have blocked the gate so that it could not be locked with a cart or a beam under some pretext, and by this means, made the entry easy to the enemy. Hannibal persuaded one to give him a castle of the Romans, and that he should feign going on a hunt at night, to show his inability to go by day for fear of the enemy, and when he returned with the game, placed his men inside with it, and killing the guard, captured the gate. You also deceive the besieged by drawing them outside the town and distant from it, by feigning flight when they assault you. And many [among whom was Hannibal] have, in addition, allowed their quarters to be taken in order to have the opportunity of placing them in their midst, and take the town from them. They deceive also by feigning departure, as did Forminus, the Athenian, who having plundered the country of the Calcidians, afterwards received their ambassadors, and filled their City with promises of safety and good will, who, as men of little caution, were short-ly after captured by Forminus. The besieged ought to look out for men whom they have among them that are suspect, but sometimes they may want to assure themselves of these by reward, as well as by punishment. Marcellus, recognizing that Lucius Bancius Nolanus had turned to favor Hannibal, employed so much humanity and liberality toward him, that, from an enemy, he made him a very good friend.

The besieged ought to use more diligence in their guards when the enemy is distant, than when he is near. And they ought to guard those places better which they think can be attacked less; for many towns have been lost when the enemy assaulted them on a side from which they did not believe they would be assaulted. And this deception occurs for two reasons: either because the place is strong and they believe it is inaccessible, or because the enemy cunningly assaults him on one side with feigned uproars, and on the other silently with the real assaults. And, therefore, the besieged ought to have a great awareness of this, and above all at all times, but especially at night, have good guards at the walls, and place there not only men, but dogs; and keep them ferocious and ready, which by smell, detect the pres-ence of the enemy, and with their baying discover him. And, in addition to dogs, it has been found that geese have also saved a City, as happened to the Romans when the Gauls besieged the Capitol. When Athens was besieged by the Spartans, Alcibiades, in order to see if the guards were awake, arranged that when a light was raised at night, all the guards should rise, and inflicted a penalty on those who did not observe it. Hissicratus, the Athenian, slew a guard who was sleeping, saying he was leaving him as he had found him. Those who are besieged have had various ways of sending news to their friends, and in order not to send embassies by voice, wrote letters in cipher, and concealed them in various ways. The ciphers are according to the desires of whoever arranges them, the method of concealment is varied. Some have written inside the scabbard of a sword. Others have put these letters inside raw bread, and then baked it, and gave it as food to him who brought it. Others have placed them in the most secret places of the body. Others have put them in the collar of a dog known to him who brings it. Others have written ordinary things in a letter, and then have written with water (invisible ink) between one line and another, which afterwards by wetting or scalding (caused) the letter to appear. This method has been very astutely observed in our time, where some wanting to point out a thing which was to be kept secret to their friends who lived inside a town, and not wanting to trust it in person, sent communications written in the customary manner, but interlined as I mentioned above, and had them hung at the gates of a Temple; which were then taken and read by those who recognized them from the countersigns they knew. Which is a very cautious method, because whoever brings it can be deceived by you, and you do not run any danger. There are infinite other ways by which anyone by himself likewise can find and read them. But one writes with more facility to the besieged than the besieged do to friends outside, for the latter cannot send out such letters except by one who leaves the town under the guise of a fugitive, which is a doubtful and dangerous exploit when the enemy is cautious to a point. But as to those that are sent inside, he who is sent can, under many pretexts, go into the camp that is besieged, and from here await a convenient opportunity to jump into the town.

But let us come to talk of present captures, and I say that, if they occur when you are being fought in your City, which is not arranged with ditches inside, as we pointed out a little while ago, when you do not want the enemy to enter by the breaks in the wall made by artillery [as there is no remedy for the break which it makes], it is necessary for you, while the artillery is battering, to dig a ditch inside the wall that is being hit, at least thirty arm lengths wide, and throw all (the earth) that is excavated toward the town, which makes embankments and the ditch deeper: and you must do this quickly, so that if the wall falls, the ditch will be excavated at least five or six arm lengths deep. While this ditch is being excavated, it is necessary that it be closed on each side by a block house. And if the wall is so strong that it gives you time to dig the ditches and erect the block houses, that part which is battered comes to be stronger than the rest of the City, for such a repair comes to have the form that we gave to inside ditches. But if the wall is weak and does not give you time, then there is need to show virtue, and oppose them with armed forces, and with all your strength. This method of repair was observed by the Pisans when you went to besiege them, and they were able to do this because they had strong walls which gave them time, and the ground firm and most suitable for erecting ramparts and making repairs. Which, had they not had this benefit, would have been lost. It would always be prudent, therefore, first to prepare yourself, digging the ditches inside your City and throughout all its circuit, as we devised a little while ago; for in this case, as the defenses have been made, the enemy is awaited with leisure and safety. The ancients often occupied towns with tunnels in two ways: either they dug a secret tunnel which came out inside the town, and through which they entered it, in the way in which the Romans took the City of the Veienti: or, by tunnelling they undermined a wall, and caused it to be ruined. This last method is more effective today, and causes Cities located high up to be weaker, for they can be undermined more easily, and then when that powder which ignites in an instant is placed inside those tunnels, it not only ruins the wall, but the mountains are opened, and the fortresses are entirely disintegrated into several parts. The remedy for this is to build on a plain, and make the ditch which girds your City so deep, that the enemy cannot excavate further below it without finding water, which is the only enemy of these excavations. And even if you find a knoll within the town that you defend, you cannot remedy it otherwise than to dig many deep wells within your walls, which are as outlets to those excavations which the enemy might be able to arrange against it. Another remedy is to make an excavation opposite to where you learn he is excavating: which method readily impedes him, but is very difficult to foresee, when you are besieged by a cautious enemy. Whoever is besieged, above all, ought to take care not to be attacked in times of repose, as after having engaged in battle, after having stood guard, that is, at dawn, the evening between night and day, and, above all, at dinner time, in which times many towns have been captured, and many armies ruined by those inside. One ought, therefore, to be always on guard with diligence on every side, and in good part well armed. I do not want to miss telling you that what makes defending a City or an encampment difficult, is to have to keep all the forces you have in them disunited; for the enemy being able all together to assault you at his discretion, you must keep every place guarded on all sides, and thus he assaults you with his entire force, and you defend it with part of yours. The besieged can also be completely overcome, while those outside cannot unless repulsed; whence many who have been besieged either in their encampment or in a town, although inferior in strength, have suddenly issued forth with all their forces, and have overcome the enemy. Marcellus did this at Nola, and Caesar did this in Gaul, where his encampment being assaulted by a great number of Gauls, and seeing he could not defend it without having to divide his forces into several parts, and unable to stay within the stockade with the driving attack of the enemy, opened the encampment on one side, and turning to that side with all his forces, attacked them with such fury, and with such virtue, that he overcame and defeated them. The constancy of the besieged has also often displeased and dismayed the besieger. And when Pompey was affronting Caesar, and Caesar's army was suffering greatly from hunger, some of his bread was brought to Pompey, who, seeing it made of grass, commanded it not be shown to his army in order not to frighten it, seeing what kind of enemies he had to encounter. Nothing gave the Romans more honor in the war against Hannibal, as their constancy; for, in whatever more inimical and adverse fortune, they never asked for peace, (and) never gave any sign of fear: rather, when Hannibal was around Rome, those fields on which he had situated his quarters were sold at a higher price than they would ordinarily have been sold in other times; and they were so obstinate in their enterprises, that to defend Rome, they did not leave off attacking Capua, which was being besieged by the Romans at the same time Rome was being besieged.

I know that I have spoken to you of many things, which you have been able to understand and consider by yourselves; nonetheless, I have done this [as I also told you today] to be able to show you, through them, the better kind of training, and also to satisfy those, if there should be any, who had not had that opportunity to learn, as you have. Nor does it appear to me there is anything left for me to tell you other than some general rules, with which you should be very familiar: which are these. What benefits the enemy, harms you; and what benefits you, harms the enemy. Whoever is more vigilant in observing the designs of the enemy in war, and endures much hardship in training his army, will incur fewer dangers, and can have greater hope for victory. Never lead your soldiers into an engagement unless you are assured of their courage, know they are without fear, and are organized, and never make an attempt unless you see they hope for victory. It is better to defeat the enemy by hunger than with steel; in such victory fortune counts more than virtue. No proceeding is better than that which you have concealed from the enemy until the time you have executed it. To know how to recognize an opportunity in war, and take it, benefits you more than anything else. Nature creates few men brave, industry and training makes many. Discipline in war counts more than fury. If some on the side of the enemy desert to come to your service, if they be loyal, they will always make you a great acquisition; for the forces of the adversary diminish more with the loss of those who flee, than with those who are killed, even though the name of the fugitives is suspect to the new friends, and odious to the old. It is better in organizing an engagement to reserve great aid behind the front line, than to spread out your soldiers to make a greater front. He is overcome with difficulty, who knows how to recognize his forces and those of the enemy. The virtue of the soldiers is worth more than a multitude, and the site is often of more benefit than virtue. New and speedy things frighten armies, while the customary and slow things are esteemed little by them: you will therefore make your army experienced, and learn (the strength) of a new enemy by skirmishes, before you come to an engagement with him. Whoever pursues a routed enemy in a disorganized manner, does nothing but become vanquished from having been a victor. Whoever does not make provisions necessary to live (eat), is overcome without steel. Whoever trusts more in cavalry than in infantry, or more in infantry than in cavalry, must settle for the location. If you want to see whether any spy has come into the camp during the day, have no one go to his quarters. Change your proceeding when you become aware that the enemy has foreseen it. Counsel with many on the things you ought to do, and confer with few on what you do afterwards. When soldiers are confined to their quarters, they are kept there by fear or punishment; then when they are led by war, (they are led) by hope and reward. Good Captains never come to an engagement unless necessity compels them, or the opportunity calls them. Act so your enemies do not know how you want to organize your army for battle, and in whatever way you organize them, arrange it so that the first line can be received by the second and by the third. In a battle, never use a company for some other purpose than what you have assigned it to, unless you want to cause disorder. Accidents are remedied with difficulty, unless you quickly take the facility of thinking. Men, steel, money, and bread, are the sinews of war; but of these four, the first two are more necessary, for men and steel find money and bread, but money and bread do not find men and steel. The unarmed rich man is the prize of the poor soldier. Accustom your soldiers to despise delicate living and luxurious clothing.

This is as much as occurs to me generally to remind you, and I know I could have told you of many other things in my discussion, as for example, how and in how many ways the ancients organized their ranks, how they dressed, and how they trained in many other things; and to give you many other particulars, which I have not judged necessary to narrate, as much because you are able to see them, as because my intention has not been to show you in detail how the ancient army was created, but how an army should be organized in these times, which should have

more virtue than they now have. Whence it does not please me
to discuss the ancient matters further than those I have judged
necessary to such an introduction. I know I should have
enlarged more on the cavalry, and also on naval warfare; for
whoever defines the military, says, that it is an army on land and
on the sea, on foot and on horseback. Of naval matters, I will not
presume to talk, not because of not being informed, but because
I should leave the talk to the Genoese and Venetians, who have
made much study of it, and have done great things in the past.
Of the cavalry, I also do not want to say anything other than what
I have said above, this part being [as I said] less corrupted. In
addition to this, if the infantry, who are the nerve of the army,
are well organized, of necessity it happens that good cavalry be
created. I would only remind you that whoever organizes the
military in his country, so as to fill (the quota) of cavalry, should
make two provisions: the one, that he should distribute horses of
good breed throughout his countryside, and accustom his men
to make a round-up of fillies, as you do in this country with
calves and mules: the other, [so that the round-up men find a
buyer] I would prohibit anyone to keep mules who did not keep
a horse; so that whoever wanted to keep a mount only, would
also be constrained to keep a horse; and, in addition, none
should be able to dress in silk, except whoever keeps a horse. I
understand this arrangement has been done by some Princes of
our times, and to have resulted in an excellent cavalry being produced in their countries in a very brief time. About other things,
how much should be expected from the cavalry, I will go back to
what I said to you today, and to that which is the custom.
Perhaps you will also desire to learn what parts a Captain ought
to have. In this, I will satisfy you in a brief manner; for I would
not knowingly select any other man than one who should know
how to do all those things which we have discussed today. And
these would still not be enough for him if he did not know how
to find them out by himself, for no one without imagination was
ever very great in his profession; and if imagination makes for
honor in other things, it will, above all, honor you in this one.
And it is to be observed, that every creation (imagination), even
though minor, is celebrated by the writers, as is seen where they

praised Alexander the Great, who, in order to break camp more secretly, did not give the signal with the trumpet, but with a hat on the end of a lance. He is also praised for having ordered his soldiers, when coming to battle with the enemy, to kneel with the left foot (knee) so that they could more strongly withstand the attack (of the enemy); which not only gave him victory, but also so much praise that all the statues erected in his honor show him in that pose.

But as it is time to finish this discussion, I want to return to the subject, and so, in part, escape that penalty which, in this town, custom decrees for those who do not return. If you remember well, Cosimo, you said to me that I was, on the one hand, an exalter of antiquity, and a censurer of those who did not imitate them in serious matters, and, on the other (hand), in matters of war in which I worked very hard, I did not imitate them, you were unable to discover the reason: to that I replied, that men who want to do something must first prepare themselves to know how to do it in order to be able afterwards to do it when the occasion permits it. Whether or not I would know how to bring the army to the ancient ways, I would rather you be the judge, who have heard me discuss on this subject at length; whence you have been able to know how much time I have consumed on these thoughts, and I also believe you should be able to imagine how much desire there is in me to put them into effect. Which you can guess, if I was ever able to do it, or if ever the opportunity was given to me. Yet, to make you more certain, and for my greater justification, I would like also to cite you the reasons, and in part, will observe what I promised you, to show you the ease and the difficulty that are present in such imitation. I say to you, therefore, that no activity among men today is easier to restore to its ancient ways than the military; but for those only who are Princes of so large a State, that they are able to assemble fifteen or twenty thousand young men from among their own subjects. On the other hand, nothing is more difficult than this to those who do not have such a convenience. And, because I want you to understand this part better, you have to know that Captains who are praised are of two kinds. The one includes those, who, with an army (well) ordered through its own natural discipline, have done great things, such as were the greater part of the Roman Citizens, and others, who have led armies, who have not had any hardship in maintaining them good, and to see to it that they were safely led. The other includes those who not only had to overcome the enemy, but before they came to this, had been compelled to make their army good and well ordered, (and) who, without doubt, deserve greater praise than those others merited who with an army which was (naturally) good have acted with so much virtue. Such as these were Pelopidas, Epaminondas, Tullus Hostilius, Phillip of Macedonia father of Alexander, Cyrus King of the Persians, and Gracchus the Roman. All these had first to make the army good, and then fight with it. All of these were able to do so, as much by their prudence, as by having subjects capable of being directed in such practices. Nor would it have been possible for any of them to accomplish any praiseworthy deed, no matter how good and excellent they might have been, should they have been in an alien country, full of corrupt men, and not accustomed to sincere obedience. It is not enough, therefore, in Italy, to govern an army already trained, but it is necessary first to know how to do it, and then how to command it. And of these, there need to be those Princes, who because they have a large State and many subjects, have the opportunity to accomplish this. Of whom, I cannot be one, for I have never commanded, nor can I command except armies of foreigners, and men obligated to others and not to me. Whether or not it is possible to introduce into them (those Princes) some of the things we discussed today, I want to leave to your judgement. Would I make one of these soldiers who practice today carry more arms than is customary, and in addition, food for two or three days, and a shovel? Should I make him dig, or keep him many hours every day under arms in feigned exercises, so that in real (battles) afterward he could be of value to me? Would they abstain from gambling, lasciviousness, swearing, and insolence, which they do daily? Would they be brought to so much discipline, obedience, and respect, that a tree full of apples which should be found in the middle of an encampment, would be left intact, as is read happened many times in the ancient armies? What can

I promise them, by which they well respect, love, or fear me, when, with a war ended, they no longer must come to me for anything? Of what can I make them ashamed, who are born and brought up without shame? By what Deity or Saints do I make them take an oath? By those they adore, or by those they curse? I do not know any whom they adore; but I well know that they curse them all. How can I believe they will observe the promises to those men, for whom they show their contempt hourly? How can those who deprecate God, have reverence for men? What good customs, therefore, is it possible to instill in such people? And if you should tell me the Swiss and the Spaniards are good, I should confess they are far better than the Italians: but if you will note my discussion, and the ways in which both proceeded, you will see that there are still many things missing among them (the Swiss and Spaniards) to bring them up to the perfection of the ancients. And the Swiss have been good from their natural customs, for the reasons I told you today, and the others (Spaniards) from necessity; for when they fight in a foreign country, it seems to them they are constrained to win or die, and as no place appeared to them where they might flee, they became good. But it is a goodness defective in many parts, for there is nothing good in them except that they are accustomed to await the enemy up to the point of the pike and of the sword. Nor would there be anyone suitable to teach them what they lack, and much less anyone who does not (speak) their language.

But let us turn to the Italians, who, because they have not wise Princes, have not produced any good army; and because they did not have the necessity that the Spaniards had, have not undertaken it by themselves, so that they remain the shame of the world. And the people are not to blame, but their Princes are, who have been castigated, and by their ignorance have received a just punishment, ignominiously losing the State, (and) without any show of virtue. Do you want to see if what I tell you is true? Consider how many wars have been waged in Italy, from the passage of King Charles (of France) until today; and wars usually make men warlike and acquire reputations; these, as much as they have been great (big) and cruel, so much more have caused its members and its leaders to lose reputation. This necessarily points out, that the customary orders were not, and are not, good, and there is no one who knows how to take up the new orders. Nor do you ever believe that reputation will be acquired by Italian arms, except in the manner I have shown, and by those who have large States in Italy, for this custom can be instilled in men who are simple, rough, and your own, but not to men who are malignant, have bad habits, and are foreigners. And a good sculptor will never be found who believes he can make a beautiful statue from a piece of marble poorly shaped, even though it may be a rough one. Our Italian Princes, before they tasted the blows of the ultramontane wars, believed it was enough for them to know what was written, think of a cautious reply, write a beautiful letter, show wit and promptness in his sayings and in his words, know how to weave a deception, ornament himself with gems and gold, sleep and eat with greater splendor than others, keep many lascivious persons around, conduct himself avariciously and haughtily toward his subjects, become rotten with idleness, hand out military ranks at his will, express contempt for anyone who may have demonstrated any praiseworthy manner, want their words should be the responses of oracles; nor were these little men aware that they were preparing themselves to be the prey of anyone who assaulted them. From this, then, in the year one thousand four hundred ninety four (1494), there arose the great frights, the sudden flights, and the miraculous (stupendous) losses: and those most powerful States of Italy were several times sacked and despoiled in this manner. But what is worse is, that those who remained persist in the same error, and exist in the same disorder: and they do not consider that those who held the State anciently, had done all those things we discussed, and that they concentrated on preparing the body for hardships and the mind not to be afraid of danger. Whence it happened that Caesar, Alexander, and all those excellent men and Princes, were the first among the combatants, went around on foot, and even if they did lose their State, wanted also to lose their lives; so that they lived and died with virtue. And if they, or part of them, could be accused of having too much ambition to rule, there never could be found in them any softness or anything to condemn, which makes men delicate and cowardly. If these things were to be read and believed by these Princes, it would be impossible that they would not change their way of living, and their countries not change in fortune. And as, in the beginning of our discussion, you complained of your organization, I tell you, if you had organized it as we discussed above, and it did not give a good account for itself, then you have reason to complain; but if it is not organized and trained as I have said, (the Army) it can have reason to complain of you, who have made an abortion, and not a perfect figure (organization). The Venetians also, and the Duke of Ferrara, begun it, but did not pursue it; which was due to their fault, and not of their men. And I affirm to now, that any of them who have States in Italy today, will begin in this way, he will be the Lord higher than any other in this Province; and it will happen to his State as happened to the Kingdom of the Macedonians, which, coming under Phillip, who had learned the manner of organizing the armies from Epaminondas, the Theban, became, with these arrangements and practices [while the rest of Greece was in idleness, and attended to reciting comedies] so powerful, that in a few years, he was able to occupy it completely, and leave such a foundation to his son, that he was able to make himself Prince of the entire world. Whoever disparages these thoughts, therefore, if he be a Prince, disparages his Principality, and if he be a Citizen, his City. And I complain of nature, which either ought to make me a recognizer of this, or ought to have given me the faculty to be able to pursue it. Nor, even today when I am old, do I think I can have the opportunity: and because of this, I have been liberal with you, who, being young and qualified, when the things I have said please you, could, at the proper time, in favor of your Princes, aid and counsel them. I do not want you to be afraid or mistrustful of this, because this country appears to be born (to be destined) to resuscitate the things which are dead, as has been observed with Poetry, Painting, and Sculpture. But as for waiting for me, because of my years, do not rely on it. And, truly, if in the past fortune had conceded to me what would have sufficed for such an enterprise, I believe I would, in a very brief time, have shown the world how much the ancient institutions were of value, and, without doubt, I would have enlarged it with glory, or would have lost it without shame.

APPENDIX

NICHOLAS MACHIAVEL,
CITEZEIN AND SECRETARIE
OF FLORENCE,
TO
THE READERS.

THE ARTE OF WARRE

NICHOLAS MACHIAVEL,

CITEZEIN AND SECRETARIE OF FLORENCE,

TO THE READERS

O thentente that such as rede this booke maie without difficultie understande the order of the battailes, or bandes of men, and of the armies, and lodgynges in the Campe, accordynge as they in the discription of theim are apoincted, I thinke it necessarie to shewe you the figure of everie one of them : wherefore it is requiset firste, to declare unto you, by what poinctes and letters, the footemen, the horsemen, and everie other particuler membre are set foorthe.

Know therfore that

· ⌐		Targetmen.
ʿ ⟩		Pikemen.
ᴗ ⌐		a Capitaine of ten men.
▼		Veliti ordinarie. ⟩ which ar those men
r ⟩		Veliti extraordinari ⟩ that shoote with har-
C ⟩		a Centurion or cap- ⟩ cabuses or bowes.
		taine of a hundred men.
k ⟩		a Constable or a captaine of a band of
	Signifieth	fower hundred and fiftie men.
H ⟩		The hed captain of a maine battel.
G ⟩		The general Captaine of the whole armie.
t ⟩		The Trompet.
d ⟩		The Drum.
b ⟩		The Ansigne.
f		The Standerde.
m ⟩		Men of Armes.
l ⟩		Light horsemen.
A ⟩		Artillerie or ordinance.

NICHOLAS MACHIAVELL

In the first figure nexte folowyng, is discribed the forme of an ordinarie battaile or bande of fower hundred and fiftie men, and in what maner it is redoubled by flanke. And also how with the verie same order of lxxx. rankes, by chaungyng onely to the hinder parte the five rankes of Pikes which were the formost of everie Centurie, thei maye likewise in bringyng them in battaile raie, come to bee placed behinde: whiche may be doen, when in marchyng, the enemies should come to assaulte them at their backes: accordynge as the orderyng therof is before declared. Fol. 87.

In the seconde figure, is shewed how a battaile or bande of men is ordered, whiche in marchyng should be driven to faight on the flanke: accordyng as in the booke is declared. Fol. 87.

In the thirde figure, is shewed how a battaile or bande of men, is ordered with two hornes, fol. 88, and after is shewed how the same maie be made with a voide place in the middest: accordynge as the orderyng therof, in the booke moste plainely is declared, fol. 89.

In the fowerth figure, is shewed the forme or facion of an armie apoincted to faight the battaile with the enemies: and for the better understandynge thereof, the verie same is plainlier set foorthe in the figure next unto it, wherby the other two figures next folowyng maie the easier be understoode: accordynge as in the booke is expressed.   Fol. 105.

In the fifte figure, is shewed the forme of a fower square armie: as in the booke is discribed.   Fol. 152.

In the sixte figure, is shewed howe an Armie is brought from a fower square facion, to the ordinarie forme, to faight a fielde: accordyng as afore is declared.   Fol. 156.

In the seventh figure, is discribed the maner of incamping: according as the same in the booke is declared. Fol. 174.

THE FIRSTE

This is the
maner of
ordering of
CCCC. men,
into lxxx.
rankes, five
to a ranke, to
bring them
into a iiii
square
battaile with
the Pikes on
the front,
as after
foloweth.

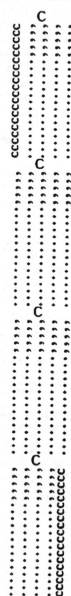

FIGURE

```
Ɔ                                    Ɔ
▼ʊ,,,,,,,,,,,,,,,,ʊ▼
▼ʊ,,,,,,,,,,,,,,,,ʊ▼
▼ʊ,,,,,,,,,,,,,,,,ʊ▼
▼ʊ,,,,,,,,,,,,,,,,ʊ▼
▼ʊ,,,,,,,,,,,,,,,,ʊ▼
▼ʊ.......d k b.......ʊ▼
▼ʊ...............ʊ▼
▼ʊ...............ʊ▼
▼ʊ...............ʊ▼
▼ʊ...............ʊ▼
▼ʊ...............ʊ▼
▼ʊ...............ʊ▼
▼ʊ...............ʊ▼
▼ʊ...............ʊ▼
▼ʊ...............ʊ▼
▼ʊ...............ʊ▼
▼ʊ...............ʊ▼
▼ʊ...............ʊ▼
▼ʊ...............ʊ▼
Ɔ ▼ ▼ ▼ ▼ ▼ ▼ ▼ ▼ ▼ ▼ Ɔ
```

This is the foresaied lxxx. rankes of iiii. C. men brought into a fower square battaile with the Pikes on the fronte. And the fiftie Veliti on the sides and on the backe.

THE SECONDE

This is the
maner of
ordering of
CCCC. men,
into lxxx.
rankes, five
to a ranke, to
bring them
into a iiii
square
battaile with
the Pikes on
the side,
as after
foloweth.

FIGURE

This is the foresaied lxxx. rankes of iiii. C. men brought into a fower square battaile with the Pikes on the side.

THE THYRDE

These are the
nombers of
rankes
appoincted to
make the
horned
battaile of,
and the
square
battaile with
the voide
space in the
middest, as
after
foloweth.

FIGURE

THE FOURTH

	A		A	A	A	A	A
I I m m ɔrCɔC	ɔʋ,,ʋCɔʋ,,ʋCɔʋ,,ʋCɔʋ,,ʋCɔʋ,,ʋCA						
I I m m r r r , , ,	▿ʋ,,ʋ▿ ▿ʋ,,ʋ▿ ▿ʋ,,ʋ▿ ▿ʋ,,ʋ▿ ▿ʋ,,ʋ▿ ▿ʋ,,ʋA						
I I m m r r r dkb	▿dkb▿ ▿dkb▿ ▿dkb▿ ▿dkb▿ ▿dkb▿						
I I t k ſ dkb , , ,	▿ʋ..ʋ▿ ▿ʋ..ʋ▿ ▿ʋ..ʋ▿ ▿ʋ..ʋ▿ ▿ʋ..ʋ▿ tG						
I I m m r r r , , ,	▿ʋ..ʋ▿ ▿ʋ..ʋ▿ ▿ʋ..ʋ▿ ▿ʋ..ʋ▿ ▿ʋ..ʋ▿ III						
k t m m r r r , , ,	▿ʋ..ʋ▿ ▿ʋ..ʋ▿ ▿ʋ..ʋ▿ ▿ʋ..ʋ▿ ▿ʋ..ʋ▿						
I ſ m m ɔrC , , ,	ɔʋ..ʋCɔʋ..ʋCɔʋ..ʋCɔʋ..ʋCCʋ..ʋɔ						
I I m m , , ,							
I I m m , , ,							
I I m m , , ,	˙˙˙˙˙ dHb ˙˙˙˙˙						
I I m m , , ,							
, , ,							
, , ,							
, , ,	ɔʋ,,ʋC		ɔʋ,,ʋC		ɔʋ,,ʋC		
, , ,	▿ʋ,,ʋ▿		▿ʋ,,ʋ▿		▿ʋ,,ʋ▿		
, , ,	▿dkb▿		▿dkb▿		▿dkb▿		
ɔdkbC	▿ʋ..ʋ▿		▿ʋ..ʋ▿		▿ʋ..ʋ▿		
, , ,	▿ʋ..ʋ▿		▿ʋ..ʋ▿		▿ʋ..ʋ▿		
, , ,	▿ʋ..ʋ▿		▿ʋ..ʋ▿		▿ʋ..ʋ▿		
, , ,	ɔʋ..ʋC		ɔʋ..ʋC		ɔʋ..ʋC		
, , ,							
, , ,							
, , ,							
, , ,							
, , ,							
, , ,							
, , ,	ɔʋ,,ʋC				ɔʋ,,ʋC		
, , ,	▿ʋ,,ʋ▿				▿ʋ,,ʋ▿		
, , ,	▿dkb▿				▿dkb▿		
˒˒˒	▿ʋ..ʋ▿				▿ʋ..ʋ▿		
dkb	▿ʋ..ʋ▿				▿ʋ..ʋ▿		
,,,	▿ʋ..ʋ▿				▿ʋ..ʋ▿		
ɔC	ɔʋ..ʋC				ɔʋ..ʋC		

¶The carriages and

FIGURE

```
      A        A        A        A        A        A
A ɔʊ,,ʊCɔʊ,,ʊCɔʊ,,,ʊCɔʊ,,ʊCɔʊ,,,ʊC        ɔCɔrC m m ll
A ᴠʊ,,ʊ ᴡ ʊ,,ʊ ᴡ ʊ,,ʊ ᴡ ʊ,,ʊ ᴡ ʊ,,ʊ ᴠ        ,,, r r r m m ll
m ᴠdkbᴡ dkb ᴡ dkb ᴡ dkb ᴡ dkb ᴠ        dkb r r r m m ll
f  ᴠʊ..ʊ ᴡ ʊ..ʊ ᴡ ʊ..ʊ ᴡ ʊ..ʊ ᴡ ʊ..ʊ ᴠ        ,,, dkb m m ll
ll ᴠʊ..ʊ ᴡ ʊ..ʊ ᴡ ʊ..ʊ ᴡ ʊ..ʊ ᴡ ʊ..ʊ ᴠ        ,,, r r r t k f ll
.. ᴠʊ..  ᴡ ʊ..ʊ ᴡ ʊ..ʊ ᴡ ʊ..ʊ ᴡ ʊ..ʊ ᴠ        ,,, r r r m m tk
   ɔʊ..ʊCɔʊ..ʊC  ..ʊCɔʊ..ʊCɔʊ..ʊC        ,,, r r r m m fl
                                               ,,,        m m ll
                dHb                            ,,,        m m ll
                                               ,,,        m m ll
                                               ,,,        m m ll
                                               ,,,
                                               ,,,
                                               ,,,
   Cʊ,,ʊɔ      ɔʊ,,ʊC      ɔʊ,,ʊC        ,,,
   ᴠʊ,,ʊᴠ      ᴠʊ,,ʊᴠ      ᴠʊ,,ʊᴠ        ,,,
   ᴠdkbᴠ      ᴠdkbᴠ      ᴠdkbᴠ        ,,,
   ᴠʊ..ʊᴠ      ᴠʊ..ʊᴠ      ᴠʊ..ʊᴠ        ɔdkbC
   ᴠʊ..ʊᴠ      ᴠʊ..ʊᴠ      ᴠʊ..ʊᴠ        ,,,
   ᴠʊ..ʊᴠ      ᴠʊ..ʊᴠ      ᴠʊ..ʊᴠ        ,,,
   Cʊ..ʊɔ      ɔʊ..ʊC      ɔʊ..ʊC        ,,,
                                               ,,,
                                               ,,,
                                               ,,,
                                               ,,,
                                               ,,,
                                               ,,,
                                               ,,,
   ɔʊ,,ʊC                  ɔʊ,,ʊC        ,,,
   ᴠʊ,,ʊᴠ                  ᴠʊ,,ʊᴠ        ,,,
   ᴠdkbᴠ                  ᴠdkbᴠ        ,,,
   ᴠʊ..ʊᴠ                  ᴠʊ..ʊᴠ        dkb
   ᴠʊ..ʊᴠ                  ᴠʊ..ʊᴠ
   ɔʊ..ʊC                  ɔʊ..ʊC        ɔC
```

the unarmed.

THE FIFT

FIGURE

THE SIXT

```
          A         A         A         A         A
mmmmmmmm CᴠCƆᴜ ,, ᴜCƆᴜ,, ᴜCƆᴜ,,ᴜCƆᴜ,,ᴜCƆᴜ,
mmmmmmmm ᴠᴠᴠᴦᴜ ,, ᴜᴦᴦᴜ,, ᴜᴦᴦᴜ,,ᴜᴦᴦᴜ,,ᴜᴦᴦᴜ,,
mmmmmmmm ᴠᴠᴠᴦᴜdkbᴜᴦᴦᴜdkbᴜᴦᴦdkbᴦᴦdkbᴦᴦᴜdk
mmmᴦkſmmm ᴠᴠᴠᴦᴜ.. ᴜᴦᴦᴜ.. ᴜᴦᴦᴜ..ᴜᴦᴦᴜ..ᴜᴦᴦᴜ..
mmmmmmmm ᴠᴠᴠᴦᴜ.. ᴜᴦᴦᴜ.. ᴜᴦᴦᴜ..ᴜᴦᴦᴜ..ᴜᴦᴦᴜ..
mmmmmmmm ᴠᴠᴠƆᴜ.. ᴜCƆᴜ.. ᴜCƆᴜ..ᴜCƆᴜ..ᴜCCᴜ.
mmmmmmmm ᴠᴠᴠƆ,,,,,C
          dkbᴦ,,,,..ᴦ                        .III
          ᴠᴠᴠᴦ,dkb..ᴦ        dHb              ..m
          ᴠᴠᴠᴦ,,,,..ᴦ        ....             ...t
          ᴠᴠᴠᴦ,,,,..ᴦ                         ....
          ᴠᴠᴠƆ,,,,..C
          ᴠᴠᴠƆ,,,,..C
          ᴠᴠᴠᴦ,,,,..ᴦ        Ɔᴜ,,  ᴜC        Ɔᴜ,,
          ƆᴠCᴦ,dkb.ᴦ         ᴦᴜ..  ᴜᴦ         ᴦᴜ,,
             ᴦ,,,,..ᴦ         ᴦᴜdkbᴜᴦ         ᴦᴜ,d
             ᴦ,,,,..ᴦ         ᴦᴜ..  ᴜᴦ         ᴦᴜ..
             ᴦ,,,,..ᴦ         ᴦᴜ..  ᴜᴦ         ᴦᴜ..
             Ɔ,,,,.C          Ɔᴜ..  ᴜC         Ɔᴜ.
             Ɔ,,,,..C
             ᴦ,,,,..ᴦ
             ᴦ,dkb..ᴦ
             ᴦ,,,,..ᴦ
             ᴦ,,,,..ᴦ
             Ɔ,,,,..C
             Ɔ,,,,..C
             ᴦ,,,,..ᴦ         Ɔᴜ,,  ᴜC
             ᴦ,dkb..ᴦ         ᴦᴜ,,  ᴜᴦ
             ᴦ,,,,..ᴦ         ᴦᴜdkbᴜᴦ
             ᴦ,,,,..ᴦ         ᴦᴜ..  ᴜᴦ
             Ɔ,,,,..C         ᴦᴜ..  ᴜᴦ
             Ɔ,,,,..C         Ɔᴜ..  ᴜC
             ᴦ,,,,.ᴦ
             ᴦ,,dkb.ᴦ
             ᴦ,,,,..ᴦ
             ᴦ,,,,..ᴦ
             Ɔ,,,,..C
             Ɔ,,,,,,C
             ᴦ,,,,,,ᴦ
             ᴦ,dkb,ᴦ
             ᴦ,,,,,,ᴦ
             ᴦ,,,,,,ᴦ
             Ɔ,,,,,,C
```

FIGURE

```
        A        A        A        A        A
, ʊCɔʊ, , ʊCɔʊ, , ʊCɔʊ, , ʊCɔʊ, , ʊCɔvɔ mmmmmmmm
, ʊrrʊ, , ʊrrʊ, , ʊrrʊ, , ʊrrʊ, , ʊrvvv mmmmmmmm
b, rr, dkb, rr, dkb, rr, dkb, rr d k brvvv mmmmmmmm
. ʊrrʊ.. ʊrrʊ.. ʊrrʊ.. ʊrrʊ.. ʊrvvv mmmrkfmmm
. ʊrrʊ.. ʊrrʊ.. ʊrrʊ.. ʊrrʊ.. ʊrvvv mmmmmmmm
. ʊCɔʊ.. ʊCɔʊ.. ʊCɔʊ.. ʊCCʊ.. ʊɔvvv mmmmmmmm
                                   ɔ..., , Cvvv mmmmmmmm
.ll..              ....            r...,, rdkb
.m.                dHb            r.dkb, rvvv
Gr..               ....            r...,, rvvv
....                               r...,, rvvv
                                   ɔ...,, Cvvv
, ʊ C              ɔʊ, , ʊC        ɔ...,, Cvvv
, ʊ r              rʊ, , ʊr        r...,, rvvv
kb, r              r, dkb, r        r.dkb, rC ɔ
, ʊ r              rʊ.. ʊr         r...,, r
, ʊ r              rʊ.. ʊr         r...,, r
, ʊ C              ɔʊ.. ʊɔ         ɔ...,, C
                                   ɔ...,, C
                                   r...,, r
                                   r.dkb, r
                                   r...,, r
                                   r...,, r
                                   ɔ...,, C
                                   ɔ...,, C
                   ɔʊ, , ʊC        r...,, r
                   rʊ, , ʊr        r.dkb.r
                   r, dkb, r        r...,, r
                   rʊ.. ʊr         r...,, r
                   rʊ.. ʊr         ɔ...,, C
                   ɔʊ.. ʊC         ɔ...,, C
                                   r...,, r
                                   r.dkb, r
                                   r...,, r
                                   r...,, r
                                   ɔ...,, C
                                   ɔ,,,,, C
                                   r,,,,, r
                                   r, dkb, r
                                   r,,,,, r
                                   r,,,,, r
                                   ɔ,,,,, C
```

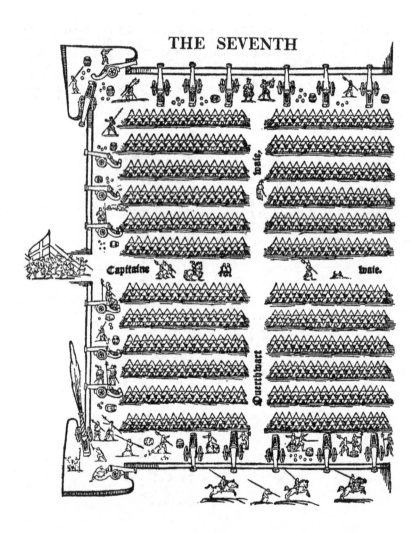

FIGURE

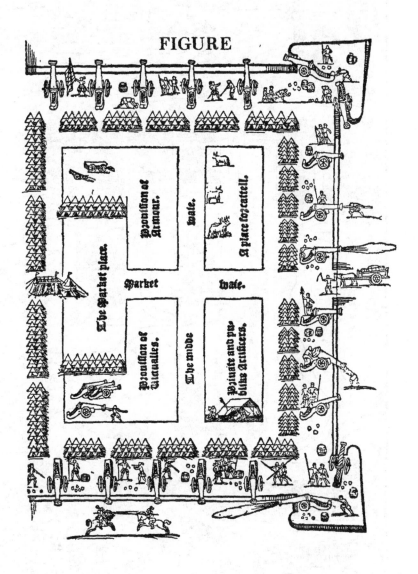

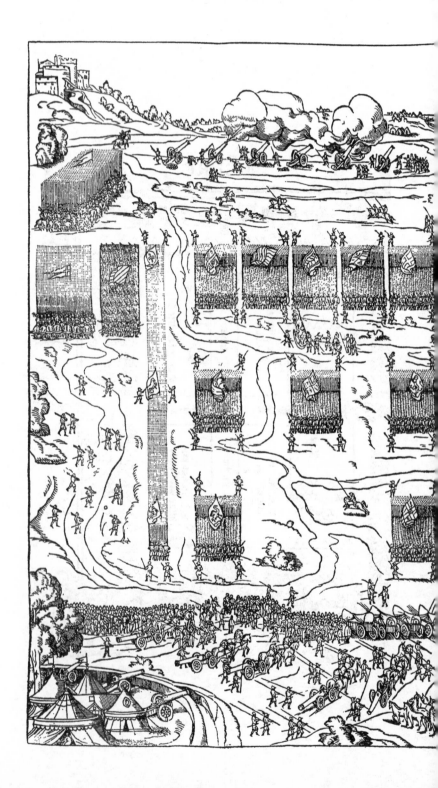

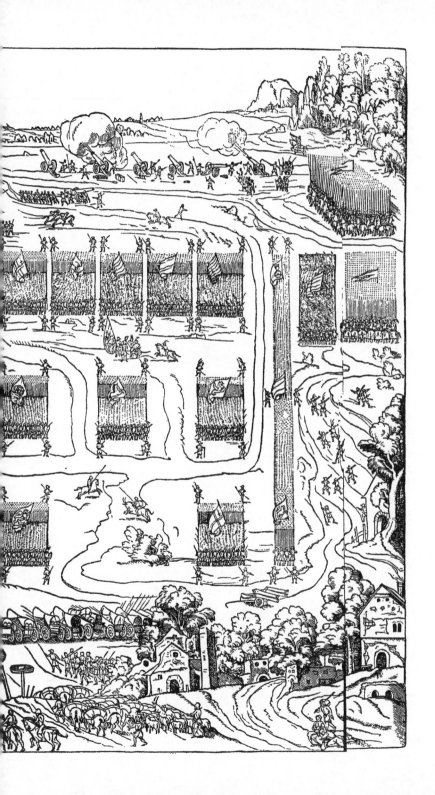